T0288915

MONTANA STATE PARKS
COMPLETE GUIDE & TRAVEL COMPANION

ERIN MADISON & KRISTEN INBODY
GREAT FALLS TRIBUNE

RIVERBEND
PUBLISHING

Copyright © 2014 by the *Great Falls Tribune*.
Published by Riverbend Publishing, Helena, Montana.

All rights reserved. No part of this book may be reproduced, stored, or transmitted
in any form or by any means without the prior permission of the publisher, except for
brief excerpts for reviews.

6 7 8 9 10 VP 23 22 21

ISBN 978-1-60639-074-0

Printed in the USA

Front cover photo: Smith River, Smith River State Park and River Corridor, by
Christopher Cauble, www.christophercauble.com
Cover and text design by Sarah Cauble, www.sarahcauble.com

RIVERBEND PUBLISHING
P.O. Box 5833
Helena, MT 59604
1-866-787-2363
www.riverbendpublishing.com

CONTENTS

ACKNOWLEDGMENTS

Visiting every state park in Montana was no small undertaking, and we couldn't have done it without the help of many.

We'd like to thank all the family and friends who joined us on our adventures. That includes our parents, who have supported both of us wherever our pursuits have taken us, our siblings and many friends, who may or may not have expected to visit state parks during road trips.

We'd also like to thank the *Great Falls Tribune* for allowing us to escape our cubicles and explore our great state. Particularly, we'd like to thank our editors, Matt Ochsner and Amie Thompson, who read each story and through their edits, made the articles better. We also owe a huge gratitude to all of our colleagues who pitched in to get this book edited.

Dayna Vik and Nick Daniels, graphics artists at the *Great Falls Tribune*, took on the task of designing the maps that appear in this book, and Nick helped shape the final product in numerous ways.

Thanks to *Tribune* publisher/editor Jim Strauss and director of business development and marketing Terry Oyhamburu for seeing the potential to turn our state parks newspaper series into a book and helping us make that a reality.

The book wouldn't have been possible without the help of the folks at Riverbend Publishing, especially publisher Chris Cauble.

Most of all, we'd like to thank everyone at Montana State Parks who helped us arrange park visits, gave us tours and answered our endless questions. Their hard work makes Montana's state parks an amazing asset to the state's residents and visitors.

Lisa and Gov. Steve Bullock with their children enjoying Montana's outdoors on a camping trip

FOREWORD BY MONTANA
GOVERNOR STEVE BULLOCK

Like most Montanans who grew up here, I have great memories from my childhood—days spent on Spring Meadow Lake, tours of Lewis & Clark Caverns, and visits to Bannack. The memories made in these state parks are something that many Montanans share, and they are something I want to pass on to my children and future generations of Montanans.

Montana has more than 50 state parks that are places where families can explore nature; enjoy camping, hiking, swimming, picnicking, fishing, boating and relaxing, or spending time learning about our state's culture and history in these amazing outdoor classrooms. Each of these parks has a unique story to tell.

The public lands that these parks are on are part of the fabric of our state. Generations of Montanans have made important memories on these lands, and we owe it to the next generation to make sure they're available for them too.

I want to congratulate Erin and Kristen for completing the "Montana State Parks Challenge," by visiting all 55 parks, and for using proceeds from this book to support our state park system. More importantly, I want to thank them for sharing their experiences with others, and hopefully inspiring them to take the challenge themselves. I know I'll be using this book to plan our family adventures this summer.

Enjoy this guidebook and use it to plan your trips to Montana's great state parks. Lisa, our kids and I look forward to seeing you and yours outdoors.

Sandstone formations glow in Medicine Rocks State Park six miles north of Ekalaka. MONTANA STATE PARKS PHOTO.

INTRODUCTION

ERIN MADISON: A road trip to a national park spawned a series of newspaper articles that eventually led to this state parks guidebook. While driving home from Yellowstone National Park, both of us mentioned that we had always wanted to visit Missouri Headwaters State Park but never had.

KRISTEN INBODY: I suggested we stop then, but you insisted we get back home and happened to be driving. Little did you realize failing to stop then would launch more than a dozen road trips around the state.

EM: An idea was born.

KI: That's right. We decided to visit all 54 Montana state parks and do a series of stories on them for the *Great Falls Tribune*.

EM: When we started our series, we wanted to call it "The Extreme Montana State Parks Challenge: Two reporters, 54 state parks, one incredible adventure."

KI: Too intense for our editors, but it was extreme. One river forded, one tick-covered dog (and two tick-covered reporters), a blizzard, an accidental detour onto icy logging roads (and another into North Dakota) and a whole lot of fun met us along the way.

EM: We managed to visit all of the parks in 11 months, crisscrossing our way across the state.

KI: Through the challenge, I fell in love with Montana all over again. Every state park was a chance to experience the state more deeply and understand a new facet. We have a gorgeous state.

EM: And now we've turned our *Tribune* series into a guide book in hopes of encouraging others to explore our incredible state parks system.

KI: The series and now the book has made me feel like a fool for all the times I've driven by and never stopped at places like Greycliff Prairie Dog Town and Tower Rock, which are so close to the interstate.

EM: I had driven past Frenchtown Pond countless times and never thought to stop. The pond doesn't look like much from the interstate, but up close, it's truly an oasis.

KI: I keep returning to Missouri Headwaters State Park. I've seen it in every season, now, and introduced the park to everyone who has happened to be in the car with me anywhere near Three Forks.

EM: We had a lot of amazing moments in our 11 months of exploring the state's parks.

KI: One of my favorite state park moments was looking out the barred jail windows in Bannack State Park to the gallows and then hiking up to them through the snow and mud. We listened to Tim Montana's "Weight in Gold," a song from the perspective of Sheriff Henry Plumber. *"Pure evil, yes I'm riding with the Devil, but I'm the only lawman that I know who's worth his weight in gold."* Creepy.

EM: We met a lot of amazing people too.

KI: Under golden-leaved trees, I chatted with blood-covered deer hunters at Hell Creek and photographed a boat launching as the sun set on Placid Lake.

EM: I've been amazed by how diverse our state park system is. I've dipped my toes into Flathead Lake, hiked to a moss-covered waterfall, ridden my bike on single-track trails and learned incredible history about Lewis and Clark. I was even able to see up close the circumference of the Anaconda Stack.

KI: I've been surprised how easy it was to work state parks into trips to other destinations. On one trip to a Bobcat football game, we stopped at Spring Meadow State Park in Helena, Elkhorn State Park near Boulder and Headwaters. It took all day to get to Bozeman, but it was a great day.

EM: You are the queen of detours.

KI: I have lived in Montana for all but a few of my 32 years and have seen every corner of the state: Yaak to Alzada, Westby to Sula. Yet this has taken me down many new roads.

EM: I've had fun taking my out-of-state family on state park adventures. It's been a great opportunity to show them some of the great things Montana has to offer.

KI: Many members of my family - sometimes unwittingly because I happened to be driving - visited state parks, too, at most 100 miles or so out of our way.

EM: We hope this book helps readers explore the state, whether it gets folks out to parks in their own town or takes them to all 54 parks and all four corners of the state.

KI: I suggest visiting all the parks in one epic road trip, which would be incredible. MapQuest suggests it would take 42½ hours of driving and 2,620 miles just to get to the nearest towns, let alone into the state parks themselves. What a big state we have.

EM: However people choose to explore the parks, we hope they'll enjoy them. And we hope they'll enjoy this book, too.

KI: We'd love to hear about all the adventures readers have while traveling to the parks. Email us at emadison@greatfallstribune.com and kinbody@greatfallstribune.com.

CAMPING AND FEES
AT MONTANA STATE PARKS

Montana residents arriving in a vehicle with valid Montana license plates are allowed to enter state parks for free. The entrance fee is paid by the $6 state parks fee included in annual vehicle registrations.

Nonresident visitors are required to pay day-use fees of $5 per car. They also can purchase a Montana State Parks annual pass for unlimited day-use access. Passes are $25 for the first vehicle, $20 for additional vehicles. The annual passes can be purchased at any state park, regional Montana Fish, Wildlife and Parks office or online at fwp.mt.gov/parks.

The America the Beautiful-National Parks and Federal Recreational Lands Pass is not valid in Montana State Parks.

Camping fees vary by season and park, but generally a campsite with electricity is $17 to $20 for residents and $25 to $28 for nonresidents (less if they have an annual pass).

Reservations can be made online in advance for Whitefish Lake, Logan, Lake Mary Ronan, West Shore, Wayfarers, Big Arm, Finley Point, Thompson Falls, Placid Lake, Salmon Lake, Beavertail Hill, Bannack, Lewis and Clark Caverns, Black Sandy, Missouri Headwaters, Cooney, Tongue River Reservoir, Makoshika, Brush Lake and Hell Creek state parks. Visit stateparks.mt.gov.

Bannack, Beavertail Hill, Lewis and Clark Caverns and Missouri Headwaters state parks offer teepee rentals. Tepees per night are $22 to $25 for residents and $30 to $35 for nonresidents.

Cabins are available to rent at Lewis and Clark Caverns. The fee is $42 to $45 for residents and $50 to $55 for nonresidents.

Big Arm State Park has yurts available that are $42 to $45 per night for residents and $50 to $60 for nonresidents.

A special permit, drawn through a lottery system, is required for the Smith River State Park and River Corridor. Permit applications are usually accepted from early January to late February, with permit results posted in early March. There is a $10 nonrefundable application fee.

MONTANA

1. Les Mason
2. Whitefish Lake
3. Lone Pine
4. North Shore
5. Logan
6. Lake Mary Ronan
7. West Shore
8. Wayfarers
9. Big Arm
10. Wild Horse Island
11. Yellow Bay
12. Finley Point
13. Thompson Falls
14. Placid Lake
15. Salmon Lake
16. Fish Creek
17. Frenchtown Pond
18. Council Grove
19. Milltown
20. Travelers' Rest
21. Beavertail Hill
22. Fort Owen
23. Painted Rocks
24. Granite Ghost Town
25. Lost Creek
26. Anaconda Stack
27. Bannack
28. Clark's Lookout
29. Beaverhead Rock
30. Lewis & Clark Caverns
31. Elkhorn
32. Spring Meadow Lake
33. Black Sandy
34. Missouri Headwaters

STATE PARKS

● Montana state park
● State park, but without public services

35. Madison Buffalo Jump	42. Sluice Boxes	49. Pictograph Cave
36. Greycliff Prairie Dog Town	43. Marias River	50. Yellowstone River
37. Cooney	44. Ackley Lake	51. Rosebud Battlefield
38. Smith River	45. Hell Creek	52. Tongue River Reservoir
39. Tower Rock	46. Brush Lake	53. Pirogue Island
40. First Peoples Buffalo Jump	47. Chief Plenty Coups	54. Makoshika
41. Giant Springs	48. Lake Elmo	55. Medicine Rocks

Placid Lake in the Seeley-Swan Valley is known for its mirror-like surface. MONTANA STATE PARKS PHOTO

GLACIER COUNTRY

LES MASON

WHITEFISH LAKE

LONE PINE

NORTH SHORE

LOGAN

LAKE MARY RONAN

WEST SHORE

WAYFARERS

BIG ARM

WILD HORSE ISLAND

YELLOW BAY

FINLEY POINT

THOMPSON FALLS

PLACID LAKE

SALMON LAKE

FISH CREEK

FRENCHTOWN POND

COUNCIL GROVE

MILLTOWN*

TRAVELERS' REST

BEAVERTAIL HILL

FORT OWEN

PAINTED ROCKS

*OPENING ANTICIPATED IN 2014

Les Mason State Park sits on the banks of Whitefish Lake in northwest Montana.

01 LES MASON

"Swim friendly."

DESCRIPTION Les Mason State Park offers access to Whitefish Lake and has the only nonmotorized public boat launch on the lake.

ACTIVITIES Boating, swimming, bird watching, fishing, picnicking

CAMPING No camping

SIZE 7 acres

SEASON Open April 1-Nov. 30. Walk-in use allowed the rest of the year

NEAREST TOWN Whitefish

FACILITIES AND SERVICES Vault toilets

DIRECTIONS From downtown Whitefish, head north on Wisconsin Avenue. Follow it as it becomes East Lake Shore Drive. The park is on the west side of the road.

CONTACT 406-752-5501 or stateparks.mt.gov/les-mason

DESCRIPTION
& HISTORY

Les Mason State Park offers a secluded, sometimes quiet spot on busy Whitefish Lake.

It offers 585 feet of sand and gravel lakeshore, as well as several picnic tables along the lakefront and a nonmotorized boat launch. Of the three public boat launches on Whitefish Lake, Les Mason is the only one that's not motorized.

The lakeshore is a short downhill walk from the parking area, which also gives the park a slightly more wild feel compared to the larger Whitefish Lake State Park, located across the lake.

"Les Mason isn't quite as developed as Whitefish," said Dave Bennetts, park manager. "It's just a day-use park."

The park, which has a nice beach, can be pretty hopping on a warm summer day.

"Les Mason is more swim friendly," Bennetts said.

It's also dog friendly, with a designated swimming area for dogs.

Les Mason closes in the winter.

"Les Mason will remain open until the snowfall limits vehicle access into the park," Bennetts said.

That means it could be open as late as the end of December depending on snow.

"Once we close the gate, the park remains open throughout the winter to foot and ski access," he said.

DON'T MISS

Head to Les Mason State Park just before sunset. The park offers beautiful views as the sun sets over the lake.

Whitefish Lake State Park offers swimming and boating on Whitefish Lake.

02 WHITEFISH LAKE

"A popular spot for waterskiing and fishing."

DESCRIPTION Whitefish Lake State Park offers access to Whitefish Lake, with shoreside camping.

ACTIVITIES Camping, boating, bird watching, fishing, swimming, picnicking

CAMPING 25 campsites. RV/trailer length limit is 40 feet. Reservations are available at stateparks.mt.gov.

SIZE 10 acres

SEASON Open year-round

NEAREST TOWN Whitefish

FACILITIES AND SERVICES Showers (open April to end of November), flush toilets, boat launch, picnic shelter, payphone, water

DIRECTIONS From downtown Whitefish, head west on West 2nd Street. Stay right onto Lion Mountain Road. Turn north onto State Park Road, which becomes West Lake Shore Drive.

CONTACT 406-752-5501 or stateparks.mt.gov/whitefish-lake

DESCRIPTION
& HISTORY

Dave Bennetts is the park manager at Whitefish Lake State Park, but the park is also a favorite recreation destination for his whole family.

"We live in town, so it's convenient," Bennetts said of the park, located on west shore of Whitefish Lake, just outside of Whitefish.

Bennetts' daughter Samantha, 4, likes to swim at the park, and his son Henry, 6, is a fan of fishing there.

Most of the summer and into early fall, the park is abuzz with campers and recreationists.

The mature forest in the Whitefish Lake State Park area gives the campsites a somewhat secluded feeling, with many sites being divided by tall trees.

Whitefish Lake State Park also offers a motorized boat launch and is a popular spot for waterskiing and fishing.

The beach at the park is very shallow, making it not so great for swimming, but the park has a designated swimming area for dogs.

Whitefish is a tourist town, so Whitefish Lake State Park is often full of visitors from across Montana, Alberta and elsewhere. Most summer nights, the campground fills up. But campers can make reservations in advance online through Montana State Park's Reserve Now program.

Whitefish Lake State Park gets a few campers throughout the winter, even though its flush toilets and shower facilities are shut down at the end of September. They reopen in early May.

DON'T MISS

Park manager Dave Bennett recommends visiting Whitefish Lake State Park in September. Most of the summer crowds are gone, but the weather is usually still fairly warm.

Lone Pine State Park overlooks the Flathead Valley, with views of Glacier National Park, Whitefish Mountain and Flathead Lake.

03 LONE PINE

"Million-dollar views."

DESCRIPTION Lone Pine State Park overlooks the Flathead River Valley, with 7.5 miles of hiking trails and a visitor center deck offering great views.

ACTIVITIES Archery, bird watching, cross-country skiing, educational exhibit, hiking, horseshoes, mountain biking, picnicking, snowshoeing

CAMPING No camping

SIZE 270 acres

SEASON Open year-round. Visitor center open Thursday-Sunday, except holidays.

NEAREST TOWN Kalispell

FACILITIES AND SERVICES Equipment rentals, grills and fire pits, maps, flush and vault toilets, water, events and children's activities

DIRECTIONS From Main Street in Kalispell, turn west onto West Center Street and then south onto South Meridian Road. At a traffic circle at the junction of U.S. Highway 98, S. Meridian Road and Foys Lake Road near Kalispell, take the Foys Lake Road exit and follow Foys Lake Road for 2.7 miles. Turn left onto Lone Pine Road and follow for one mile to 300 Lone Pine Road.

CONTACT 406-755-2706 or stateparks.mt.gov/lone-pine

DESCRIPTION
& HISTORY

Million-dollar views set Lone Pine State Park apart.

"That's one of the biggest draws. It's probably the most accessible and best view of the valley," said Amy Grout, park manager. "Accessibility is a huge draw for folks."

From the deck of the visitor center and a trail's lookout, visitors can see high peaks in Glacier, Whitefish Mountain, Flathead Lake, the Flathead River and everything between on a clear day.

"I never get over the view from the main overlook," Grout said. "It's always breathtaking no matter the time of day or time of year. There's something almost magical about it. I've seen it with immersions and fog in the valley, with vibrant colors in the summer and yellow canola fields below."

On the Fourth of July, about 300 people come to the park to watch fireworks in the valley.

The state park was part of a large sheep ranch. Ernest and Hazel White donated the land in 1941 for public use and education.

"To think of something like that during that time is pretty awesome," Grout said. "What a great resource we have today because of their forethought."

Kalispell's sprawl surrounds much of the park, which now stands as an oasis.

The visitor center, redesigned in 2007, focuses on co-existing with wildlife, from bear-proofing yards to preventing the spread of noxious weeds.

DON'T MISS

Follow a trail that begins in the parking lot to the overlook for an excellent view of the Flathead River Valley.

A bridge connects the visitor center to trails through the park.

"We have so many neighbors in that interface and get bears right down to Kalispell," Grout said. "We've got a lot of close experiences within the valley that we can speak to. The grizzly in the display is one that got in trouble."

Grout said she hopes the display helps visitors realize they can make a difference in the lives of the wildlife with which they share the land.

Park trails can accommodate long or short hikes.

"The great thing is we don't have one trail that goes for seven and a half miles," Grout said. "We have lots of trails that make up the route. People can make a different route every day. You can take an hour or two and see a bunch of different trails."

Visitors will notice that there is far more than one lone pine growing at Lone Pine State Park.

"It looks a little different now than it did when the land was deeded to Montana," Grout said. "There was still more than just one, but the park's name comes from the fact that at one of the main overlooks there was a single pine that stood alone, crooked and growing out of a cliff. It was a sentinel pine that gave Lone Pine Hill its name long before it was a state park and was a landmark for travelers coming up the valley."

The tree eventually succumbed to gravity, but its former location is marked with a plaque.

"I get that question a lot," Grout said. "People say, 'You have a lot of trees around here. Really, 'Lone' Pine?'"

The Lone Pine State Park visitor center has information on making the most of the park and on coexisting with wildlife.

North Shore State Park on the north end of Flathead Lake is an undeveloped park. MONTANA STATE PARKS PHOTO

04 NORTH SHORE

"The spring migration can be really impressive."

DESCRIPTION North Shore State Park sits on the north end of Flathead Lake. It's managed jointly as a state park and wildlife management area and is a great place to see upland birds and wildlife.

ACTIVITIES Bird watching, wildlife watching

CAMPING No camping

SIZE 350 acres

SEASON Closed March 1-July 15 during nesting season

FACILITIES AND SERVICES None

NEAREST TOWN Somers

DIRECTIONS North Shore State Park is located along the north shore of Flathead Lake. From Somers, head east on Highway 82 for about 4.5 miles. The park will be on the south side of the highway.

CONTACT 406-752-5501

DESCRIPTION
& HISTORY

North Shore State Park, on the north end of Flathead Lake, is a great place to see upland birds, waterfowl and other wildlife.

The park is managed both as a state park and wildlife management area, located north of Flathead Lake between Montana Highway 82 and the U.S. Fish and Wildlife Service's Flathead Lake Waterfowl Production Area.

"It's a really cool spot," said Dave Landstrom, parks manager for state parks in northwest Montana.

The park and WMA border the federal waterfowl production area, which stretches all the way across Flathead Lake's north shore.

"That whole top of the lake is a federal waterfowl production area," he said.

The park is managed primarily as a WMA without any amenities or services.

"It's access for you to do self exploration," Landstrom said. "You're not going to go there and find a visitor center or trails or camping," he said.

The main draw of the park is bird watching. Visitors can walk across the park and WMA land to reach the federal land, looking for birds along the way.

"You can get down into some really beautiful, quiet places," Landstrom said, with views of the lake on one side and the mountains on the others.

A wide range of birds can be spotted at North Shore State Park including eagles, raptors, osprey, avocet and others.

"The whole spectrum of open country and wetland avian life is there," Landstrom said. "We'll see snowy owls wintering here."

DON'T MISS

Dave Landstrom suggests visiting North Shore State Park in the spring when the waterfowl migration is at its peak. It's a great place to see pintails, swans and other birds.

"The spring migration can be really impressive there," he said. "Sometimes you'll see thousands of pintail ducks there."

Montana Fish, Wildlife and Parks purchased the first parcel of land, 160 acres in size, in 2009. At the time it was agricultural land.

"Currently the property looks an awful lot like ag land elsewhere in the valley," Landstrom said.

However, the goal is to transform it back to a more natural habitat.

"The idea is to slowly convert that to upland bird and waterfowl habitat," he said.

In 2014, FWP purchased another 190-acre piece of land next door.

The goal of that acquisition was to protect ground water, surface water and wetlands on and near Flathead Lake, which in turn would help improve or maintain the high water quality of Flathead Lake.

Initially, Montana State Parks had plans to develop a campground at the site, but those plans are now on hold.

North Shore State Park borders the federal waterfowl production area, which stretches all the way across Flathead Lake's north shore. MONTANA STATE PARKS PHOTO

Logan State Park sits on the banks of Middle Thompson Lake.

05   LOGAN

"Most of the visitors are locals in the know."

DESCRIPTION Logan State Park offers access to the north shore of Middle Thompson Lake, with a campground, picnic area and playground.

ACTIVITIES Swimming, boating, camping, water-skiing and fishing

CAMPING 37 campsites, RV/trailer length limit is 40 feet. Reservations are available at stateparks.mt.gov.

SIZE 17 acres

SEASON Open year-round

FACILITIES AND SERVICES Flush toilets, shower, RV dump station, RV hookups, boat launch

NEAREST TOWN Happy's Inn

DIRECTIONS The park is located just off Highway 2, halfway between Kalispell and Libby, about five miles east of Happy's Inn.

CONTACT 406-752-5501 or stateparks. mt.gov/logan

DESCRIPTION
& HISTORY

Located halfway between Libby and Ka-lispell, Logan State Park is popular with residents of both northwest Montana towns.

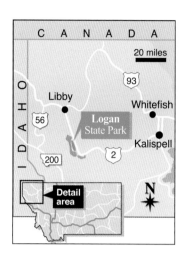

"It seems to be more of a local-use state park," park manager Dave Bennetts said.

Rather than attracting out-of-state tourists, most of Logan's visitors are locals in the know.

The park, with frontage on the north shore of Middle Thompson Lake, offers swimming, boating, camping, water-skiing and fishing.

Fishing and boating are the main draws, Bennetts said.

"Out there, folks are fishing for salmon and pike," he said. "There's some bass in there, some trout and perch. It's got a little bit of everything."

Come December, Middle Thompson Lake usually freezes over.

"Then the ice fishing takes over from there," Bennetts said.

Logan State Park is 17 acres but sits in the middle of the Thompson Chain of Lakes, a fishing access site complex that offers nearly 3,000 acres of public land on 18 lakes stretching 20 miles.

"The state park is literally right in the middle of that chain of lakes," Bennetts said.

DON'T MISS

Plan to camp a night or two at Logan State Park. Located in a fairly untraveled part of the state, Logan offers quiet escape with beautiful scenery.

Logan State Park offers 37 campsites. The campground includes a swing set, horseshoe pit and a short nature trail. There are another 90 campsites along the chain of lakes.

"The chain of lakes camping is a little more primitive camping," Bennetts said.

Logan State Park's campground offers a few more luxuries, including a shower house that is open from April to the end of November.

The park is located in a heavily forested area, surrounded by western larch, Douglas fir and ponderosa pine. Tree-covered mountains give the lake a beautiful backdrop.

Rick and Kristy Dieterich of Thompson Falls walk their cocker spaniels at Lake Mary Ronan State Park, seven miles west of Flathead Lake.

06 LAKE MARY RONAN

"It's off the beaten path."

DESCRIPTION Lake Mary Ronan State Park offers a chance to camp and fish at a quiet mountain lake away from the bustle of Flathead Lake.

ACTIVITIES Bird/wildlife watching, boating, canoeing, fishing, hiking, picnicking, swimming, showshoeing

CAMPING 25 campsites, plus group camping space. Reservations are available at stateparks.mt.gov.

SIZE 120 acres

SEASON Open year-round

NEAREST TOWN Dayton

FACILITIES AND SERVICES Bear-resistant storage lockers, boat launch/dock, grills/fire rings, vault toilets, water, electricity

DIRECTIONS From U.S. Highway 93 at Dayton, travel west seven miles on Lake Mary Ronan Road.

CONTACT 406-752-5501 or stateparks.mt.gov/lake-mary-ronan

DESCRIPTION
& HISTORY

For Rick Dieterich, Lake Mary Ronan State Park is an oasis in every season.

He comes to the park to ice fish in winter and to camp in May, July and August.

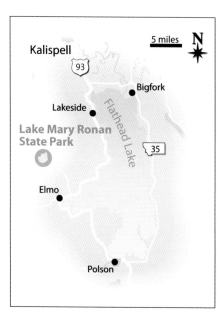

As he and wife, Kristy, walked their cocker spaniels, Yeti and Neesha, to the shore, the Thompson Falls couple reflected on the calm and beauty of the water.

"We like it," Rick Dieterich said. "It's a beautiful place and close enough to come here. There aren't many places in Montana to fish for salmon."

The park is a quiet yet popular spot, especially among anglers like Dieterich, said Amy Grout, park manager.

"It gets pretty busy and stays that way through the summer," Grout said. "They hit it hard in the end of May and June as a good fishing month."

Kokanee salmon fishing is a huge draw for visitors to the park. Lake Mary Ronan also has yellow perch and small-mouth bass.

"Even though the state park has a lot of fishing use, it is a very peaceful park," Grout said. "It's off the beaten path, and we always have really respectful users who want to enjoy the woods, enjoy nature. A lot have been coming for years, and they just love that lake."

Two private camps, a few private homes and lots of public land surround the lake.

"That appeals to folks. They can camp and explore the Forest Service land and fish on a beautiful lake," Grout said. "There is a lot to do beyond the state park. It's a neat place."

DON'T MISS

Look for wildflowers, wildlife, mushrooms and huckleberries in the forest, depending on the season.

Just less than two miles of hiking trails offer another recreation opportunity at the park. The well-marked road to the state park is paved and passes through a scenic valley of red barns, fields and views of the lake.

"It's gorgeous back there, and there isn't traffic. You can really enjoy the scenery," Grout said. "In that valley, I always see lots of birds of prey. Every different species you can think of, and it's really active."

Grout spotted a great gray owl, perhaps warming and drying himself after a storm.

"It was so crazy," she said. "That was pretty impressive."

The state park has been getting busier in recent years with the addition of paved roads and electricity to the 25-site campground, plus an improved group camping area. The park has a boating ramp and boat trailer parking, too.

"It's really increased the desirability of those sites," Grout said. "It used to be pretty dusty when people drove around the camp loop. Since that time, people have realized this is a nice place."

Even when it's full on summer weekends, the campground remains quiet and removed from highway noise.

The park, which sits at an elevation of 3,770 feet, freezes early.

"It's awesome for ice fishing, with derbies held, too," Grout said.

Anglers love Lake Mary Ronan State Park for its fine fishing, with salmon, yellow perch and smallmouth bass among the species in the lake.

West Shore State Park is a great place to access Flathead Lake. MONTANA STATE PARKS PHOTO

07 WEST SHORE

"There's a little bit for everybody."

DESCRIPTION West Shore State Park sits on the west shore of Flathead Lake, offering boating, camping and general lake access.

ACTIVITIES Camping, boating, bird watching, fishing, hiking, picnicking, swimming

CAMPING 31 campsites, 7 are tent only; RV/trailer size limit is 40 feet. Reservations can be made in advance at stateparks.mt.gov.

SIZE 129 acres

SEASON Open year-round

NEAREST TOWN Lakeside

FACILITIES AND SERVICES Vault toilets, RV hookups, boat launch, water

DIRECTIONS West Shore State Park is located on Highway 93, which runs along the west shore of Flathead Lake, about 5 miles south of Lakeside.

CONTACT 406-752-5501 or stateparks.mt.gov/west-shore

DESCRIPTION
& HISTORY

Winter or summer, you can expect to find activity at West Shore State Park, about five miles south of Lakeside.

"It gets a fair amount of use (in winter)," said Amy Grout, park manager.

And, of course, in the summer, it's a popular spot for swimming, boating, water skiing and picnicking.

West Shore State Park is unique compared to the other six state parks on Flathead Lake thanks to its hilly topography. West Shore offers approximately 4 miles of hiking trails through those hills.

"They're all single-track dirt trails," Grout said.

Some of the trails are steep, while others contour the hillside.

"There's kind of a little bit for everybody," Grout said. "And of course there are beautiful views of the lake at different points."

The park also offers a boat ramp that is accessible in the winter, reaching far enough into the lake that boats can launch even when the water is low.

West Shore State Park offers 31 campsites, some of which are available in the winter. Seven of those sites are for tents only and offer great views of the lake, Grout said.

DON'T MISS

Wander around on the West Shore's trail system. You'll be treated to some nice hiking and beautiful views of the lake.

Wayfarers State Park sits on Flathead Lake moments away from the town of Bigfork.

08 WAYFARERS

"A great place to watch the sunset."

DESCRIPTION Located on the northeast shore of Flathead Lake, Wayfarers State Park offers public access to the lake, as well as camping.

ACTIVITIES Camping, boating, bird watching, fishing, hiking, picnicking

CAMPING 30 campsites, 7 of which are for tents only. The maximum length for RV/trailers is 50 feet. Reservations can be made in advance at stateparks.mt.gov.

SIZE 67 acres

SEASON Open May 1-Sept. 30

FACILITIES AND SERVICEs Flush toilets, boat launch, grills and fire rings, picnic shelter, showers, RV hookups, water

NEAREST TOWN Bigfork

DIRECTIONS Wayfarers State Park is located on Highway 35, which runs along the east shore of Flathead Lake. It's just south of Bigfork.

CONTACT 406-752-5501 or stateparks. mt.gov/wayfarers

DESCRIPTION & HISTORY

Friends Linda Chehard and Ginny Larson have a unique way of enjoying Wayfarers State Park, just outside Bigfork on the shore of Flathead Lake.

"We come here and knit once a week," Chehard said.

The friends bring camp chairs and their knitting supplies, find a sunny spot on the lake shore and enjoy a view while crafting shawls, vests and scarves.

"It's our tranquility for the week," Larson said.

Wayfarers State Park is one of seven state parks on Flathead Lake.

On the lake's northeast shore, Wayfarers is a great place to watch the sunset.

Wayfarers is by far the most visited of Flathead's state parks, with 112,000 people coming to the park in 2012.

Wayfarers, which opens for the season May 1, is within walking distance of downtown Bigfork. It offers 30 campsites, seven of which are walk-in, tent-only sites.

The park also has walking paths through the rocky lake shore and mature forests and a boat ramp.

DON'T MISS

Stay at one of the seven tent-only campsites at the park. They're slightly secluded and off the beaten path.

The sun sets over Flathead Lake. MONTANA STATE PARKS PHOTO

Big Arm State Park offers camping on the west shore Flathead Lake.

09 BIG ARM

"The campground is right on the water."

DESCRIPTION Big Arm State Park sits on the west shore of Flathead Lake, offering boating, camping and general lake access.

Activities Camping, boating, bird watching, fishing, hiking, picnicking, swimming

CAMPING 7 tent sites, 41 RV/trailer sites; size is limited to 30 feet. Reservations can be made in advance at stateparks.mt.gov.

SIZE 217 acres

SEASON Open year-round

NEAREST TOWN Polson

FACILITIES AND SERVICES Flush toilets, showers, boat launch, water, picnic shelter

DIRECTIONS Big Arm State Park is located on Highway 93, which runs along the west shore of Flathead Lake, about 14 miles north of Polson.

CONTACT 406-752-5501 or stateparks. mt.gov/big-arm

DESCRIPTION
& HISTORY

Big Arm State Park's long pebble beach is popular with sunbathers and swimmers. Big Arm also offers a boat launch, picnic shelter, a 2.5-mile hiking trail and camping.

"Big Arm is more of a tradition-al camping area," said Jerry Sawyer, park manager. "The campground is right on the water."

The 48-site campground offers no electrical or water hookups.

The hiking trail provides nice views of surrounding moun-tain ranges. Those who are lucky enough may spot some birds or other wildlife when they explore the park.

Flathead Lake offers excellent fishing opportunities, but anglers should note that a joint state/tribal fishing license is needed to fish at this park.

In addition to traditional camping, Big Arm State Park offers a 20-foot-wide, 10-foot-tall yurt available for rent.

Campground reservations and yurt reservations can be made at stateparks.mt.gov.

DON'T MISS

Rent the yurt for a unique camping experience. The round structure has electrical outlets, lights, electric heat and a propane barbecue for outdoor cooking.

A network of trails makes it easy to explore Wild Horse Island.

10 WILD HORSE ISLAND

"Excellent wildlife viewing opportunities."

DESCRIPTION Wild Horse Island State Park is the largest island on Flathead Lake. A herd of wild horses lives on the island, as well as bighorn sheep and other wildlife.

ACTIVITIES Boating, bird watching, fishing, hiking, picnicking, wildlife viewing, swimming

CAMPING No camping

SIZE 2,163 acres

SEASON Open year-round

FACILITIES AND SERVICES Vault toilets

NEAREST TOWN Polson

DIRECTIONS Wild Horse Island is only accessible by boat. Shuttles are available out of several Flathead Lake communities. The closest public boat launches are Big Arm State Park near Elmo and Walstad Fishing Access Site about three miles east of Big Arm State Park. Wild Horse Island is about four or five miles from those boat launches.

CONTACT 406-752-5501 or stateparks. mt.gov/wild-horse-island

DESCRIPTION & HISTORY

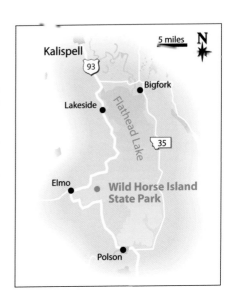

With much of the shore of Flathead Lake lined by multi-million dollar houses, businesses and marinas, Wild Horse Island State Park is a sharp contrast.

The 2,163-acre island located near the lake's Big Arm area is almost completely undeveloped.

"We manage this as a primitive area," said Jerry Sawyer, Wild Horse Island State Park manager. "We don't provide picnic tables or a boat dock."

Despite the lack of amenities, Wild Horse Island State Park is a popular destination. Some 18,000 people visit the island each year, mainly between May and September.

The island offers excellent wildlife viewing opportunities including bighorn sheep, deer, eagles and even a herd of wild horses.

Wild Horse Island is currently home to six of its namesake animals. The oldest of the herd recently died.

"He was an old-timer," Sawyer said, about 30 years old, which is very old for a wild horse.

Montana State Parks maintains a wild horse herd on the island by transplanting horses there. However, the name goes back to a legend saying that area tribes used to swim their horses out to the island to hide them from raiding tribes because horses were extremely valuable.

"I don't know if that's accurate or not," Sawyer said.

If that legend holds true, a few horses were likely left behind when the risk of raids had subsided and the tribes took their animals back to the mainland. In 1855, the Stevens expedition, which was surveying the area, caught sight of horses on the island and named the body of land Wild Horse Island.

DON'T MISS

Wild Horse Island State Park manager Jerry Sawyer's favorite time to visit the island is April or May, when the grass is lush and green, wildflowers are in bloom and summer tourists have yet to arrive.

Whenever you go, wander around the trails on the island. If you're lucky you'll spot the wild horses or a few bighorn sheep.

Those original wild horses are long gone. The island's current herd comes from the BLM's wild horse adoption program, which allows people or agencies to adopt wild horses from areas where the animals are overpopulated.

A few years ago, the Wild Horse Island herd was dying off, so State Parks moved four new wild mares to the island. Park officials didn't know it, but one of those horses was pregnant and later gave birth to a colt. Most of the island's horses are solid colored, but the colt came out spotted.

"This one's a paint," Sawyer said.

The horses generally stay grouped together, and the herd often can be spotted by visitors. Feeding the horses is strictly prohibited.

Since the early 1900s, Wild Horse Island has changed ownership numerous times. Hikers still will see a few buildings left over from homesteading days. The island was farmed, and there's an apple and pear orchard that still produces fruit.

"If you catch it at the right time of the summer, you don't have to pack a lunch," Sawyer said.

The island became a state park in 1978.

Wild Horse Island is the largest island in a freshwater lake west of Minnesota and is almost entirely state owned.

"We do have private lots on the island," Sawyer said.

Some homestead buildings remain on Wild Horse Island.

Look for the wild horses that inhabit Wild Horse Island, but don't approach or feed them.

Wild Horse Island is also home to a healthy herd of bighorn sheep. One of the island's owners brought a few sheep over.

"That's what started the herd up," Sawyer said.

Bighorn sheep currently number about 200. Sheep are periodically removed from the island to keep the population in check.

Wild Horse Island is accessible by boat only. There are six established landing sites, with information kiosks and trailheads that offer access to the island's interior. However, visitors can beach their boats anywhere on the island's public shoreline.

The island has strict rules that pets and bicycles aren't allowed to prevent spooking the wildlife, and smoking and fires are prohibited because of fire danger. The island is for day use only; camping is prohibited. Groups can't exceed 15.

Visitors should pack out their own trash. There is one compost toilet on the island near Skeeko Bay; otherwise, people should dig cat holes.

The island has about four miles of trails built in an inter-connecting loop system. Visitors also can go off trail.

Wild Horse Island State Park is open and usually accessible year-round. A visitor who comes in the middle of winter likely will have the park all to himself.

Yellow Bay State Park's pebble beach makes it a nice place to swim on Flathead Lake.

11 YELLOW BAY

"It's got a nice swimming beach."

DESCRIPTION Located on the east shore of Flathead Lake, Yellow Bay State Park has a nice beach for swimming, as well as a boat launch.

ACTIVITIES Boating, fishing, water skiing, bird watching, swimming, camping

CAMPING 4 tent campsites. Open for camping May 1-Sept. 30

SIZE 15 acres

SEASON Open year-round

FACILITIES AND SERVICES Flush toilets, boat launch, grills and fire rings, water, picnic shelter

NEAREST TOWN Big Fork

DIRECTIONS Yellow Bay State Park is located about 8 miles south of Big Fork on Highway 35, which runs along the east shore of Flathead Lake.

CONTACT 406-752-5501 or stateparks. mt.gov/yellow-bay

DESCRIPTION & HISTORY

Yellow Bay is one of seven state parks located on Flathead Lake, but each state park on the lake is unique.

"They do have their own character," said Jerry Sawyer, manager of Yellow Bay State Park.

Yellow Bay is a smaller, less developed park. It offers four tent camping sites, but is primarily a day-use park.

"It's got a nice swimming beach," Sawyer said. "That's primarily the draw there."

Yellow Bay also offers a steep boat ramp, which allows boaters to access the lake, even when water levels are low in the winter months. The park is open year-round.

Yellow Bay is surrounded by cherry, apple, pear and other fruit orchards. Fruit can be purchased at roadside stands, and some orchards offer people the chance to pick their own fruit.

Yellow Bay, like the other state parks on Flathead's shore, gives the public access to a lake that is mostly private.

"There's not a whole lot of public access to Flathead Lake," Sawyer said. "Most of the shoreline is developed."

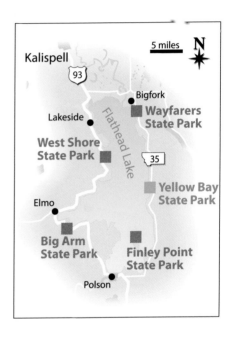

DON'T MISS

Pack a picnic lunch for your visit to Yellow Bay State Park. The park has a nice picnic shelter on the lakeshore.

David Juhl sets out in his pontoon boat across Placid Lake in the Seeley-Swan Valley.

14 PLACID LAKE

"Has an away-from-it-all feeling."

DESCRIPTION Placid Lake State Park can be a beautiful retreat for a weekend of fishing or an afternoon picnicking and playing in the water.

ACTIVITIES Bird/wildlife watching, boating, fishing, picnicking, swimming, water skiing

CAMPING 40 campsites. Reservations are available at stateparks.mt.gov.

SIZE 31 acres

SEASON 7 a.m. to 10 p.m., May 1-Nov. 30

NEAREST TOWN Seeley Lake

FACILITIES AND SERVICES Boat launch, grills/fire rings, RV hookups, shower, picnic shelter, vault and flush toilets

DIRECTIONS From Seeley Lake, travel south on Montana Highway 83. Turn right onto North Placid Lake Road. After .5 miles, take the first right to stay on North Placid Lake Road for 1.3 miles. Continue on Placid Lake Road for .9 miles, and then turn left onto South Placid Lake Road.

CONTACT 406-677-6804 or stateparks. mt.gov/placid-lake

DESCRIPTION
& HISTORY

As Shirley and David Juhl launched their pontoon boat into water turned pink and orange by the setting sun, Shirley said the view of the Swan Range makes Placid Lake especially beautiful.

Near Salmon Lake State Park on a tributary of the Clearwater River, 31-acre Placid Lake State Park has a smaller boat launch and great scenery. Though the lake is known for its smooth water, it's named for New York's Lake Placid.

Tucked in a dense coniferous forest, the park has an away-from-it-all feeling that belies its easy access.

Placid Lake has 40 campsites, but they close at the end of September. The recent addition of showers and laundry facilities has added some cushiness to the camping experience.

Among state parks of the Missoula area, this park is one of the most popular, with about 40,000 visitors every summer, sharing the lake, campground, volleyball courts and horseshoe pit.

Boat slips rental are available on a first-come, first-serve basis.

Former logging roads circle the lake and offer a path for hiking or mountain biking.

Osprey, loons, necked grebes and waterfowl are among the birds that make the lake a home.

DON'T MISS

Placid Lake State Park has interpretive displays on early logging practices in the valley, with massive western larch stumps attesting to the former use of the land.

Salmon Lake State Park is a popular spot in the Seeley-Swan Valley and just about 10 minute's drive from Clearwater Junction.

15 SALMON LAKE

"Piercingly beautiful."

DESCRIPTION Salmon Lake State Park offers water access, a forest to explore and a base in the beautiful Seeley-Swan Valley.

ACTIVITIES Bird/wildlife watching, boating, fishing, hiking, picnicking, swimming, waterskiing

CAMPING 20 campsites. Reservations are available at stateparks.mt.gov.

SIZE 42 acres

SEASON Open May 1 to late October, with day use only in October

NEAREST TOWN Seeley Lake

FACILITIES AND SERVICES Boat launch, RV hookups and dump station, shower, flush and vault toilets, picnic shelters

DIRECTIONS The park is 7.7 miles south of Seeley Lake along Montana Highway 83.

CONTACT 406-677-6804 or stateparks. mt.gov/salmon-lake

DESCRIPTION
& HISTORY

As the evening sunlight sparkles golden on Salmon Lake, many visitors feel it must be the most glorious place in Montana at that moment.

"It's piercingly beautiful sometimes," said Cathy Morris, a campground host at Salmon Lake State Park with her husband, Richard.

Salmon Lake State Park is an easily accessible spot for picnics, boating, fishing, hiking and camping.

Just off Montana Highway 83, Salmon Lake State Park was a gift of the Champion Timberlands Corp. to honor three foresters who died in a plane crash in 1976. A memorial plaque is near the park's center.

The large day-use area has a swimming area and two docks, a nature trail, paved parking and picnic shelters. The beach is gravel.

Loons, osprey, great blue herons, red-necked grebes, bald eagles and other birds make the site worth a stop, and the fall colors are fantastic at their peak.

DON'T MISS

Walk along the gravel shoreline in the early morning or evening for the best bird and wildlife viewing.

Salmon Lake State Park offers camping among western larch, ponderosa pine, and Douglas fir trees.

Afternoon watersports give way to calm evenings at Salmon Lake State Park.

Fish in the lake and Clearwater River include rainbow, brown, bull and cutthroat trout, as well as whitefish, perch, northern pike, and, of course, kokanee salmon.

Near the main day-use area, the campground has a small day-use area.

Most weeks of the summer, the campground is full, so reservations are highly recommended.

Western larch, ponderosa pine and Douglas fir lend their shade. The park's 20 camp spots are paved and have electrical hookups, plus "all the good things people really want," Richard said.

The showers are about dozen years old, but they're so well cared for they look new. The whole campground is well maintained and clean.

"It's such a nice campground, quiet and family-friendly," Richard said. "Until I was a host, I think we'd never known there was a campground here, but the word is getting out."

Some campers use Salmon Lake as a base for hikes to Holland Falls or Morrell Falls. The Morrell Lake Trail is about two miles long and is a National Recreation Trail.

In the summer, interpretive programs at the amphitheater featuring experts in wildlife, legends and other topics draw attendees from throughout the valley.

The creek for which the park is named flows through Fish Creek State Park, located west of Missoula.

16 FISH CREEK

"Fishing is a huge draw."

DESCRIPTION In a beautiful mountain setting, Fish Creek State Park offers opportunities for hiking, fishing, mountain biking and wildlife viewing.

ACTIVITIES Hunting, hiking, wildlife viewing, photography, snowshoeing, picnicking

CAMPING No camping

SIZE 5,603 acres

SEASON Open year round

FACILITIES AND SERVICES None

NEAREST TOWN Alberton

DIRECTIONS The park is 35 miles west of Missoula. From Interstate 90, take exit 66 and turn south on Cyr-Iron Mountain Road. Follow that for 3.5 to 4 miles to the park, which is undeveloped so it lacks signs and amenities.

CONTACT 406-542-5500 or stateparks. mt.gov/fish-creek

DESCRIPTION
& HISTORY

From Williams Peak, visitors to Fish Creek State Park can take in spectacular views of the Bitterroot Mountains to the southwest and the Mission Mountains to the northeast.

"It's a beautiful spot," said Mike Hathaway, park manager.

Not surprisingly, fishing is a huge draw to one of Montana's newest state parks.

Fish Creek State Park is bordered by Fish Creek on the eastern side of the park and the Rock Creek drainage on the western side. The park is just off the Clark Fork River. Cold water fisheries, the creeks host trout and are especially known for bull trout.

Alberton Gorge, which has a good regional reputation, is adjacent to the park on its northern boundary.

"The Alberton Gorge River Coordinator has been a very popular area for many years for white-water rafting and kayaking," Hathaway said. "It's continuing to gain popularity."

The state park was part of a 41,000-acre, $17 million land acquisition from Plum Creek Timber Co. by the Nature Conservancy and Trust for Public Lands. The state officially gained ownership of the land in 2010, with a share set aside for the state park.

The state park's 5,603 acres, only 30 minutes west of Missoula, are used for hunting, hiking, wildlife viewing, photography, snowshoeing, firewood gathering and berry-picking. Its lands include timbered draws, ridges, a few flat stretches, riparian areas and steep, narrow canyons.

DON'T MISS

Park manager Mike Hathaway's favorite hike in the park is to the base of the Williams Peak Fire Lookout Tower. Reaching the lookout tower at the summit of Williams Peak, elevation 5,400 feet, requires a hike of about a mile from the Forest Service road on the western edge of the park.

The way Fish Creek will be developed is still a matter of discussion for the new state park.

Hathaway said his favorite things to do at the park are hiking and sight-seeing.

"If you're lucky enough to hike to Williams Peak, you have terrific views of the surrounding countryside, and there are some neat hiking opportunities along Fish Creek, as well as beautiful spots overlooking the Rock Creek drainage," he said.

"I've heard of folks riding mountain bikes. The property has quite a legacy of logging roads on it, about 60 miles worth," he said.

Fish Creek State Park is undeveloped and lacks signs and amenities, but plans are in the works to develop the park. The parks system recently went through a public scoping process to understand what people wanted to see at Fish Creek.

The plan likely will identify easy initial projects such as erecting orientation signs. Eventually, campgrounds and other facilities could be added.

Snow dusts moss growing along Fish Creek, a fast-moving creek popular with anglers and kayakers.

Frenchtown Pond State Park is a great place for a picnic.

17 FRENCHTOWN POND

"A popular place no matter the season."

DESCRIPTION Frenchtown Pond is a small, spring-fed lake that is stocked with fish and offers swimming and nonmotorized boating opportunities.

ACTIVITIES Boating, bird watching, fishing, swimming, picnicking, ice skating

CAMPING No camping

SIZE 41 acres

SEASON Open year round

NEAREST TOWN Frenchtown

FACILITIES AND SERVICES Flush toilets, picnic shelter, water, grills and fire rings

DIRECTIONS From Missoula, take Interstate 90 west. Take exit 89 for Frenchtown. Turn right onto Demer Street and left onto Frenchtown Frontage Road, which leads to the park.

CONTACT 406-542-5500 or stateparks.mt.gov/frenchtown-pond

DESCRIPTION & HISTORY

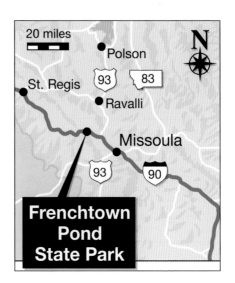

Frenchtown Pond State Park is a popular place no matter what the season.

The park is especially busy in the summer with swimming, fishing and nonmotorized boating.

"The park is packed with kids of all ages enjoying the water," said Mike Hathaway, manager at Frenchtown Pond State Park.

It's popular with kayakers and swimmers, and the Garden City Triathlon is held there every year.

"There are even sailboats that come out here," said Becky Wikum, a regular visitor to the state park.

In the winter, the pond is used for ice skating and ice fishing.

The pond typically freezes over with ice thick enough to be walked on by early January or so.

"We get a fair amount of ice fishing and skating at the pond," Hathaway said. "There are folks out there all year long."

DON'T MISS

Visit Frenchtown Pond in January or February and bring your ice skates. The pond usually freezes solid as a great place for skating.

The pond is spring-fed and 22 acres in size with a maximum depth of 15 feet, said Mike Hathaway, manager at Frenchtown Pond State Park.

The park itself is about 40 acres, and offers picnic shelters and playground equipment. It's a day use-only park.

Another unique use of the pond is SCUBA diving. The local dive club uses the pond for practice and cleans up the bottom of the pond while they're at it, Hathaway said.

Montana Fish, Wildlife and Parks stocks the pond with large-mouth bass and occasionally trout from the Arlee hatchery.

FWP's fishery division also recently worked to improve bass habitat by sinking trees in the pond.

The pond is visible from Interstate 90, but driving by on the interstate doesn't do the pond justice.

"It's not as small as what you would imagine," Wikum said.

Tall old-growth ponderosa pines trees grow in Council Grove State Park.

18 COUNCIL GROVE

"Nice place to just relax."

DESCRIPTION Council Grove State Park, located on the banks of the Clark Fork River, is the location where the Hellgate Treaty was signed, creating the Flathead Indian Reservation.

ACTIVITIES Hiking, bird watching, fishing, picnicking, history

CAMPING No camping

SIZE 187 acres

SEASON Open year-round during daylight hours

NEAREST TOWN Missoula

FACILITIES AND SERVICES Vault toilets, water

DIRECTIONS Take Mullan Road west out of Missoula. Follow the road about seven miles to the park.

CONTACT 406-542-5500 or stateparks.mt.gov/council-grove

DESCRIPTION & HISTORY

Located on the banks of the Clark Fork River, with groves of old-growth ponderosa pines, Council Grove State Park has a solemn, tranquil atmosphere.

Just seven miles outside Missoula, the state park offers open space for recreation, while also being a place of historical significance.

Most visitors use the park for walking or hiking or exercising their dogs, park manager Mike Hathaway said.

"We get a lot of folks who come out to walk their dogs," he said.

What those visitors may not realize is that Council Grove was the site of the signing in 1855 of the Hellgate Treaty, which created the Flathead Indian Reservation.

The treaty, negotiated between the U.S. government and the Salish, Kootenai, and Pend d'Orielle tribes, was signed at the site July 16, 1855.

The tribes were reluctant to sign the treaty but believed it guaranteed their rights to be self-governing. Eventually, the treaty resulted in the last of the Salish being removed under military force from their traditional homelands in the Bitterroot Valley, south of Missoula.

Park managers aren't sure how the location was selected as the treaty signing site, although some historians argue that the treaty actually was signed at a site down river, Hathaway said.

DON'T MISS

Explore the park's web of trails, many of which lead to the river.

Council Grove State Park sits on the banks of the Clark Fork River just west of Missoula.

Council Grove is a nice place to watch the changing seasons. In the spring, the park is speckled with wildflowers. In the fall, the cottonwoods change colors, and winter offers a unique snow-covered beauty.

In the summer, it's a popular place to access the river.

"A lot of folks come to dip their feet in the water or to just cool off," Hathaway said. "It's fairly close to Missoula, so we get a lot of folks just coming out to enjoy the solitude. It has almost a solemn or a reverent feeling to it with those big ponderosa pines there."

Council Grove features a monument with the full text of the treaty and some historical information about the treaty, the site and the Native American tribes involved.

"It's really kind of a nice place to just relax and contemplate," Hathaway said.

Visitors at Council Grove State Park stop to look at the monument marking the location where the Hellgate Treaty was signed in 1855 creating the Flathead Indian Reservation.

Milltown State Park marks the spot where the Milltown Dam once stood. The dam and the pollution behind it were removed and the park is part of rehabilitation efforts along the river.

19 MILLTOWN

"Montana's newest state park."

DESCRIPTION Milltown State Park is located at the newly restored confluence of the Clark Fork and Blackfoot rivers, where the Milltown Dam used to be located.

ACTIVITIES Bird watching, fishing, hiking, picnicking, history

CAMPING No camping

SIZE 535 acres

SEASON An overlook area opened in 2011 and is open year round. The main area of the park is expected to open in 2014 or 2015

NEAREST TOWN Milltown/Bonner

FACILITIES AND SERVICES The overlook area does not have toilet facilities. There is a paved parking lot and interpretive signs.

DIRECTIONS To reach the overlook, take Highway 200/Interstate 90 Frontage Road east out of Missoula. After passing through East Missoula, turn south onto Speedway Avenue and then east on to Deer Creek Road. Follow the road about three miles to the overlook.

CONTACT 406-542-5500 or stateparks. mt.gov/milltown

DESCRIPTION
& HISTORY

For 100 years, a dam blocked the confluence of the Clark Fork and Blackfoot rivers. That dam was removed in 2008, allowing the two rivers to flow together as they had for thousands of years before. Now the confluence of those rivers is the future site of Montana's newest state park.

Michael Kustudia, manager of the park, often finds himself stopping and looking around the future site of Milltown State Park and thinking about the history that has taken place there.

"I just imagine standing in one place and imagine a time lapse," he said. "It's just a very special place in terms of all the history."

Long before Milltown Dam was built in 1908, the area was covered by the water of Glacial Lake Missoula. Later, it was a passage way for Native Americans. Wildlife also has long used it as a corridor. Meriwether Lewis passed through and described the confluence area on July 4, 1806. Lewis even discovered the monkey flower in a spot Kustudia believes to be within the park boundaries. The Mullan Expedition also passed through.

Later, when the area became industrialized, that narrow spot between the mountains and the river was a hotbed of activity, seeing the development of the railroad, interstate, power lines and other infrastructure.

When Milltown State Park opens in 2014 or 2015, Kustudia hopes the park will tell all of those stories, while also offering hiking trails and river recreation.

Milltown Dam was completed in 1908, built by copper king William Clark, to produce electricity for a lumber mill in Bonner.

"Once upon a time, it powered most of western Montana," Kustudia said.

DON'T MISS

The only portion of the park that is open before late 2014 or 2015 is the overlook. It offers an excellent view of the Clark Fork and Blackfoot rivers and their confluence.

June 1908 saw a massive flood, washing all kinds of mining waste downstream from Butte. Much of that waste, made up of chemicals and heavy metals, ended up behind Milltown Dam. Over time, river silt covered it up, and eventually in 1981, arsenic was found in the ground water.

In 2006, work began to remove the dam and the sediments behind it. A working group was formed to help make redevelopment plans for the area.

"The capstone was going to be the new state park," he said.

When that park opens, it will include 535 acres, stretching from the river's flood plain up the surrounding hillsides.

An overlook opened in 2011 that offers visitors a view of the confluence of the Clark Fork and Blackfoot rivers and the former location of the dam.

The main portion of the park will be located near the confluence of the two rivers, near where the dam once stood. Much of the future state park once sat under the water of the reservoir created by the dam.

"Telling the story of the industrial past without sugar coating it or demonizing it, that's kind of the challenge," Kustudia said.

The overlook at Milltown State Park offers a view of the confluence of the Clark Fork and Blackfoot rivers.

The amphitheater at Travelers' Rest State Park is used frequently. The park offers interpretative programs daily in the summer, with special events held throughout the year.

20   TRAVELERS' REST

"The only verified campsite of Lewis and Clark."

DESCRIPTION Travelers' Rest State Park is the only archaeologically verified campsite of the Lewis and Clark expedition.

ACTIVITIES Hiking, bird watching, fishing, picnicking, history, education

CAMPING No camping

SIZE 51 acres

SEASON Open year round. Closed Thanksgiving, Christmas and New Year's Day

NEAREST TOWN Lolo

FACILITIES AND SERVICES Gift shop, picnic shelter and tables, flush toilets, running water

DIRECTIONS From Missoula, take Highway 93 south to Lolo. Turn west onto Highway 12 and look for the park on the south side of the road.

CONTACT 406-273-4253 or stateparks.mt.gov/travelers-rest

DESCRIPTION
& HISTORY

Travelers' Rest State Park offers visitors a chance to walk in the footsteps of Lewis and Clark. It's the only archaeologically verified campsite of Lewis and Clark's entire expedition.

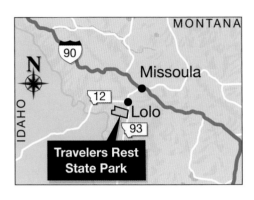

"Or in the whole universe, as we like to say," said Loren Flynn, Travelers' Rest park manager.

Travelers' Rest, located near Lolo, was donated to Montana State Parks in 2001, after which time an archeological investigation revealed that Lewis and Clark camped on the site both in 1805 and again in 1806 on their return trip.

Archeologists found many clues that led them to determine Travelers' Rest was the exact campsite.

"It really was a preponderance of evidence," Flynn said.

The archeologists started by measuring the magnetic properties of the soil at the site and found what they called anomalies, basically spots where the soil had changed. Through excavation, they found a piece of lead, a trade bead, areas that had been used as cook or campfires and even a latrine.

"The archeologists discovered that Lewis and Clark were following a military manual that gave specifications as to the layout of a campsite," Flynn said.

The hearths, latrines and other findings matched the layout prescribed in the manual.

The charcoal found in the hearths was carbon dated and matched the time Lewis and Clark would have been there, give or take 30 years. The trace elements in the lead matched those that would have come from the source in Kentucky from which Lewis and Clark likely would have gotten lead.

DON'T MISS

Grab a walking tour pamphlet from the visitor center and take a self-guided walking tour along the park's half-mile interpretive trail. The tour points out specific areas used by the Lewis and Clark expedition. Better yet, ask a volunteer to share some of the park's history.

"Lewis and Clark were doing some gun making and probably bullet making here in 1806," Flynn said.

The archeologists even found traces of mercury vapor in the camp's latrine area.

"(Mercury) was a common medical treatment at the time," Flynn said.

Before leaving on the expedition, Clark went to Philadelphia and studied with a doctor who was a proponent of using mercury, which acts as a laxative, to treat nearly any ailment.

"Lewis left Philadelphia with about 600 of those pills," Flynn said. "It was a cure all. They took it for pretty much everything."

Prior to that excavation work, the National Park Service had designated a National Historic Landmark where it was thought the expedition had camped.

"It was just about a mile to the east of us," Flynn said.

Historians knew Lewis and Clark camped near Lolo but thought it was closer to the confluence of Lolo Creek and the Bitterroot River.

The archeologists submitted their work to the National Park Service, which, after a thorough review, agreed to move the historic landmark to the state park.

"Obviously there needed to be a really compelling reason to change that geographic boundary," Flynn said.

For centuries, Native Americans also used the area that is now Travelers' Rest State Park as a campsite and trail junction.

Now part of the state park is designated as a national historic landmark.

Even before Travelers' Rest became the first archaeologically verified Lewis and Clark campsite, historians identified it as an important spot. It was a critical decision point for the expedition both on the way west and the return.

After camping there from Sept. 9 to 11, 1805, the expedition made the decision to take the overland route over Lolo Pass.

"It was a really important decision point when they came here in 1805," Flynn said."They recognized it as the most direct route to the Pacific."

On the return, they camped at the site from June 30 to July 3, 1806.

"When they left Travelers' Rest they went their separate ways and were apart for about six weeks," Flynn said.

Before Lewis and Clark, Travelers' Rest was long used by Native Americans as a trade and cultural center.

"Because of where it's located, at this pretty major crossroads of trails, it was a major trade center," Flynn said. "It was a major stopping point and pass-through point for a lot of people."

Travelers' Rest State Park has an active volunteer corps that leads programs, staffs the visitor center and wanders the park's trails, offering a deeper explanation of the site's history.

In addition to the park's rich history, Travelers' Rest is a great place for bird watching, wildlife viewing and fishing in Lolo Creek, Flynn said.

Visitors wander through Travelers' Rest State Park outside Lolo.

Beavertail Hill State Park borders the Clark Fork River, allowing for easy recreation access.

21 BEAVERTAIL HILL

"A wonderfully diverse park."

DESCRIPTION Beavertail Hill State Park is a retreat just off Interstate 90 for those who need a camping spot or a leg stretch.

ACTIVITIES Bird/wildlife watching, boating, education, fishing, hiking, picnicking

CAMPING 28 campsites and tepee rentals. Reservations are available at stateparks. mt.gov.

SIZE 65 acres

SEASON Open May 1-Oct. 31

NEAREST TOWN Clinton

FACILITIES AND SERVICES Grills/fire rings, picnic shelter, flush and vault toilets

DIRECTIONS The park is 26 miles east of Missoula and 10.7 miles east of Clinton. Take Exit 130 off Interstate 90 and travel south for .3 miles on Bonita Station Road.

CONTACT 406-677-6804 or stateparks. mt.gov/ beavertail-hill

DESCRIPTION
& HISTORY

A creek-side camping spot, a nature walk and a fishing opportunity in the Clark Fork River are attractions at Beavertail Hill State Park.

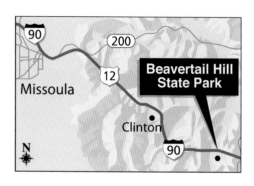

"When I look at that park, I don't know who it can't satisfy," said Ryan Sokoloski, park manager. "I love it. It is amazing, a wonderfully diverse park."

The park offers the chance to bird watch, canoe, hike and picnic.

"It's a great place to swing off the road, walk the dogs, get fresh air," Sokoloski said. "People who have a limited timeframe and want to experience nature without driving forever, they can have that wild outdoor experience."

The park's name comes from the resemblance of a hill to the west to a beaver. However, now the "tail" is bisected by the interstate.

Day-use of the park gives visitors a chance to fish, play horseshoes, have a picnic or float a stretch in the Clark Fork.

One of the best features for noncampers is the self-guided nature trail, which points out natural features through the park's riparian setting. The whole route could take an hour, but visitors can join and leave the path at many points.

Cottonwoods, ponderosa pine and Douglas fir provide shade throughout the park.

While at the park, take note of the old Chicago, Milwaukee and St. Paul

DON'T MISS

Cross the park to see the Clark Fork River along the eastern boundary.

Stopping to walk the one-mile self-guided nature trail is a good way for travelers on Interstate 90 to stretch their legs.

Railroad tracks. Cities sent mail, farmers sent wheat and loggers sent timber along the abandoned railroad just north of the state park. Passengers went both ways on what was once the only mainline from Chicago to the Pacific Northwest.

"Those tracks once ran through the park," Sokoloski said. "There's early pioneering history there."

The park's amphitheater in the pines hosts a junior ranger program on Saturdays and a summer interpretive series at 8 p.m. every other Friday.

Fishing opportunities are available in the Clark Fork River at Beavertail Hill State Park.

The east barracks are the only original remaining structure at Fort Owen State Park.

22 FORT OWEN

"It was a very prominent feature on the landscape."

DESCRIPTION Fort Owen was home to Montana's first Catholic church, the state's first permanent white settlement and Montana's first sawmill, first grist mill, first agricultural development, first water right and the first school for settlers.

ACTIVITIES History, photography, picnicking

CAMPING No camping

SIZE One acre

SEASON Open year round. Open 8 a.m.-9 p.m. May 1-Aug. 31 and 9 a.m.-5 p.m. Sept. 1-April 30

NEAREST TOWN Stevensville

FACILITIES AND SERVICES Vault toilets

DIRECTIONS Travel south from Missoula on Highway 93. Head east about one half mile on the Stevensville Cutoff Road. The park is on the left. The park is surrounded by private property and the turn can be easily mistaken for a private road.

CONTACT 406-273-4253 or stateparks. mt.gov/fort-owen

DESCRIPTION & HISTORY

John Owen is an important but little-known figure in Montana's history.

Originally from Philadelphia, Owen moved to Montana, and in 1850, purchased a mission near Stevensville that had been established by Jesuit priests.

Owen transformed the mission into a trading post, dubbing it Fort Owen.

"I think his vision was Fort Owen and the Bitterroot Valley would be the hub of western Montana," said Vernon Carroll, interpretive ranger for Montana State Parks.

The fort had tall adobe whitewashed walls. One trader described it in his journal as gleaming in the distance.

"It was a big very prominent feature on the landscape," Carroll said.

Fort Owen was established before Missoula. The nearest structure as large as the fort was in Saint Paul or Salt Lake City.

As Owen worked to establish his fort, it became home to Montana's first sawmill, first grist mill, first agricultural development, first water right and the first school for settlers. It was also home to Montana's first Catholic church, founded by Father DeSmet in 1841, before Owen took ownership.

Some say Fort Owen was Montana's first permanent white settlement. Others would argue that Fort Benton in northcentral Montana deserves that title. Fort Owen was a continuous unbroken presence between the establishment of St. Mary's Mission in 1841 through the establishment of Fort Owen in 1850, continuing to the town of Stevensville in the 1860s, Carroll explained. Fort Benton was established in 1846.

DON'T MISS

Be sure to go inside east barracks, the only original structure in the park, and the historic cabin. Both are furnished and offer interpretive signs.

Owen's vision of Fort Owen being the hub of western Montana didn't last long.

When the Mullan Road was built, connecting Fort Benton to Walla Walla, Wash., it became the main transportation route and bypassed Fort Owen.

"It went through what is now Missoula," Carroll said.

Later a railroad was built along the same route.

"(Owen) kind of got left out of the whole thing," Carroll said.

By the mid-1860s, Missoula had become the prosperous part of the valley, and by the 1870s, Owen was having health and financial problems.

"Toward the end of his time there, he was struggling financially," Carroll said. "It was no longer the center of commerce in Montana."

Some historians say Owen went insane, others say he was struggling with alcoholism or dealing with what we now know as Alzheimer's or dementia.

"He couldn't manage the affairs of the fort anymore," Carroll said.

Owen mortgaged the fort, and later, ownership was transferred to Washington McCormick, to whom Owen owed money.

"It was not a priority for (McCormick)," Carroll said. "The fort basically fell into disrepair."

Owen was forced to leave Montana and was sent back to Philadelphia to live with relatives. He died there in 1889.

McCormick also died that same year at Fort Owen. He was repairing a roof at the fort when a windstorm blew off the roof.

The fort came to be owned by local farmers and ranchers who donated it to the Stevensville Historical Society. Eventually it was donated to Montana State Parks.

Today, visitors can see the outline of the fort's walls, along with a reconstructed root cellar, well house and historic cabin.

The east barracks are the only original structure still remaining at the site.

"The back wall and a portion of the sidewalls and the interior walls are the original adobe," Carroll said.

Visitors can see the charcoal and straw that was used in the adobe to give it structural integrity.

The one-acre state park is surrounded by private property, and visitors are encouraged to be sensitive to that private property. No camping is allowed at the park.

Fort Owen is open every day year round. Staff is there on occasion to answer questions, but it's mainly a self-guided experience with interpretive signs explaining the fort's history.

Painted Rocks State Park gets its name from the green, yellow and orange lichens that cover the surrounding granite and rhyolite cliffs.

23 PAINTED ROCKS

"Short season but a great place to be."

DESCRIPTION A reservoir in the West Fork Valley of the Bitterroot Mountains.

ACTIVITIES Camping, boating, bird watching, fishing, hiking, swimming, picnicking

CAMPING 25 campsites with a 25-foot length limit for RVs and trailers

SIZE 23 acres

SEASON Open year round

NEAREST TOWN Darby

FACILITIES AND SERVICES Vault toilets, boat launch, picnic shelter

DIRECTIONS Painted Rocks State Park is located about 30 miles south of Darby. To get there, follow Highway 93 south out of Darby. After about 5 miles, head southwest on the West Fork Road. Follow it about 25 miles to the state park.

CONTACT 406-273-4253 or stateparks. mt.gov/painted-rocks

DESCRIPTION & HISTORY

The prime season at Painted Rocks State Park is short, but during that time, the park, on the West Fork of the Bitterroot River on the banks of a reservoir, is a popular place.

"It's a short season, but when you can take advantage of it, it's a great place to be," said Loren Flynn, park manager.

The reservoir, located in the Bitterroot Mountains, is drawn down starting in August and is covered by ice for most of the winter. The lake starts to fill in the spring and is usually in great shape by Memorial Day.

Painted Rocks State Park offers a 25-site campground, a boat ramp and a dock. It's popular with boaters, water skiers and anglers, who take advantage of the reservoir and the river below the dam.

"The West Fork of the Bitterroot is really popular with float fishermen," Flynn said.

Visitors also will find numerous trail heads near the park that offer access to national forest land in the Bitterroot Mountains.

The park and reservoir are named Painted Rocks for the green, yellow and orange lichens that cover the surrounding granite and rhyolite cliffs.

Those lichens aren't rare; they're just very prominent in the area, Flynn explained.

Painted Rocks Dam was built in 1939 by the Montana Water Conservation Board for agricultural use. Today, the reservoir provides water for irrigation, stockwater, domestic use and stream flows for fish.

Visitors to the park may be treated to a view of the many species of wildlife that live in the area including elk, deer, black bear, moose, osprey, great blue heron,

DON'T MISS

Before you arrive at the state park, you'll drive past the dam that creates Painted Rocks Reservoir. Stop at the dam overlook and take in the view.

water ouzels, spotted sandpiper and kill-deer. They may even catch a glimpse of bighorn mountain sheep or peregrine falcons, both of which were re-introduced to the area in the 1980s.

The Lewis and Clark expedition passed through the area in 1805. Later, the valley became an important corridor for fur companies, as well as the "mountain men" of the era.

Long before that, the West Fork of the Bitterroot, like the rest of the Bitterroot Valley, was used by the Salish people as a hunting area, as well as a place to gather other foods, including huckleberries, serviceberries, bitterroot and trout.

Painted Rocks State Park, located about 30 miles south of Darby, offers a 25-site campground, a boat ramp and a dock.

Visitors explore the Lewis and Clark Caverns by candlelight during a special December tour.
MONTANA STATE PARKS PHOTO

SOUTHWEST MONTANA

GRANITE GHOST TOWN

LOST CREEK

ANACONDA STACK

BANNACK

CLARK'S LOOKOUT

BEAVERHEAD ROCK

LEWIS AND CLARK CAVERNS

ELKHORN

SPRING MEADOW

BLACK SANDY

Granite Ghost Town State Park, near Philipsburg, was once a booming mining town with some 3,000 residents.

24 GRANITE GHOST TOWN

"One of the largest silver mines in the world."

DESCRIPTION Granite was a booming silver mining town in the 1890s with a population of 3,000 people. After the mine went bust, nearly all the residents left, but visitors can still see the old ruins of buildings and mining structures.

ACTIVITIES Photography, wildlife viewing, history, hiking opportunities on the surrounding Forest Service land

CAMPING No camping

SIZE Half acre

SEASON Open May 1 to Sept. 30, daylight hours

NEAREST TOWN Philipsburg

FACILITIES AND SERVICES None

DIRECTIONS From downtown Philipsburg, head south on South Montgomery Street. Veer East onto Galena Street, which will turn into Granite Road. Follow signs to the state park.

CONTACT 406-287-3541 or stateparks.mt.gov/granite-ghost-town

DESCRIPTION
& HISTORY

Peeking inside the ruins of the Miners' Union Hall in Granite Ghost Town State Park, it's fun to imagine the sights and sounds of the building during its heyday.

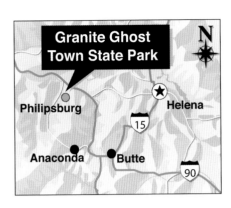

The two-story hall, with its maple dance floor, once was known as the finest dance hall in the Northwest, said Roger Semler, assistant administrator for Montana State Parks.

Although only a few buildings in ruin remain, Granite's Main Street also was home to saloons, a newspaper office, rooming houses and restaurants.

At its peak, upward of 3,000 miners lived in Granite. The town was large enough to have its own Chinatown and red-light district.

Today, it's a true ghost town. No one lives at the site. Some buildings remain. Visitors also can find stone walls, scrap metal and shards of glass and porcelain around the site.

"It's a typical mining town that went from boom to bust," Semler said.

Silver was first discovered in the Granite area in 1865. The town boomed around 1875 when miners uncovered a silver "bonanza."

"A lot of literature will claim it was one of the largest silver mines in the world," Semler said. "There are probably some people down in Colorado who might argue against that."

Largest in the world or not, the mine yielded some $40 million in silver.

"There was probably some wealth made there, and probably a lot of people didn't become wealthy," he said.

The mine nearly closed before anyone struck it rich. Before the miners hit the payload, the mine's backers de-

DON'T MISS

Plan time to hike the web of trails that lead to various old homes and other ruins in the area, and stop to look at some of the mines and structures that line the winding road on the way to Granite.

cided the venture was hopeless and sent a telegram telling the miners to shutter the mine. That telegram was delayed en route, and the miners uncovered the bonanza before the telegram arrived.

The mine shut down after the silver panic of 1893 and was never mined again.

Granite Ghost Town State Park is just more than half an acre in size with two buildings – the Union Hall and the superintendent's house – on the site.

Visitors will see other buildings, tailing and mine remnants in the area. Some of those sit on private land, while others are on Forest Service land.

Most of the buildings are in poor shape, but visitors can go inside some, Semler said.

About five miles from Philipsburg, the ghost town makes a nice side trip for those visiting the area. The road to Granite gains 1,280 feet in elevation, winding up a nearby mountain side.

"It's narrow in spots," Semler said. But a passenger car can make the trip when the road is in good conditions.

"In the spring, snow does tend to linger on the road leading up there," Semler said.

Little remains of the old Miner's Union Hall at Granite Ghost Town State Park. The two-story building was once known as the finest dance hall in the northwest.

The plentiful aspen trees at Lost Creek State Park near Anaconda make fall a beautiful time to visit the park.

25 LOST CREEK

"There's plenty of elbowroom."

DESCRIPTION Lost Creek State Park offers camping, hiking and wildlife watching opportunities in a scenic canyon, along with a beautiful waterfall.

ACTIVITIES Camping, bird watching, fishing, hiking, picnicking, wildlife viewing

CAMPING 25 campsites. RV/trailer size is limited to 23 feet

SIZE 502 acres

SEASON Open May 1-Nov. 30

NEAREST TOWN Anaconda

FACILITIES AND SERVICES Vault toilets, water

DIRECTIONS From Interstate 90, take Exit 201 for Warm Springs. Head west on the I-90 Frontage Road and veer onto Montana 48 South. After about 5.7 miles, turn north onto Galen Road. After 2 miles, turn west on Lost Creek Road. Follow the road 6 miles to the park.

CONTACT 406-287-3541 or stateparks. mt.gov/lost-creek

DESCRIPTION
& HISTORY

Visitors to Lost Creek State Park are greeted by limestone cliffs that rise higher and higher as the canyon floor narrows.

"It's a beautiful canyon," said Mike Hathaway of Montana State Parks. "You're up in the Flint Creek Mountain Range."

The canyon walls, made of igneous and sedimentary rock, rise 1,200 feet above the canyon floor.

The park often offers views of mountain goats and bighorn sheep.

"It's a beautiful place, even if you don't see sheep," Hathaway said.

Hundreds of elk and bighorn sheep live in the area year-round. Bighorn sheep were transplanted to Lost Creek in 1967 from the Augusta area.

The park is particularly spectacular in the fall when the leaves are changing colors.

"Fall is a really good time to visit Lost Creek because of the aspen," Hathaway said.

Lost Creek makes an excellent place to camp.

"It's just a wonderful campground," Hathaway said. "It's fairly remote, so it's not that crowded."

The 25 campsites are all fairly large and are popular for camping trips with extended families.

"There's plenty of elbowroom for folks," Hathaway said.

At the far end of the campground, visitors can find the trailhead for a short paved path that leads to Lost Creek Falls, which are "very pretty tumbling falls," Hathaway said.

Those looking for a longer hike can opt to take the U.S. Forest Service trail that starts in the park. That trail leads hikers to a main ridge trail that runs through the Flint Creek Range.

DON'T MISS

Take the short hike from the campground to Lost Creek Falls. Look for the trailhead at the far end of the campground. Walking to the scenic falls only takes about five minutes on a paved path and is worth the walk.

The state park is 502 acres, but it joins some 12,000 acres of state and federal land, creating important wildlife habitat.

The gate to Lost Creek is closed every year on Nov. 30, and usually by that time there's a fair amount of snow on the road, Hathaway said.

After Nov. 30, visitors can ski or snowshoe into the park. Lost Creek reopens May 1.

Visitors to Lost Creek State Park near Anaconda can follow a short trail to Lost Creek Falls.

A sculpture at the Anaconda Stack State Park highlights the area's mining history.

26 ANACONDA SMOKE STACK

"Taller than the Washington Monument."

DESCRIPTION Anaconda Smoke Stack State Park offers a viewing area to see the stack that helped carry off smoke and gases produced as byproducts of copper smelting, as well as interpretive signs explaining the history of the Anaconda Copper Company.

ACTIVITIES History, photography

CAMPING No camping

SIZE 10 acres, only 2.2 are accessible

SEASON Open year-round

FACILITIES AND SERVICES Interpretive displays

NEAREST TOWN Anaconda

DIRECTIONS The park is located on the west end of Anaconda at 100 Smelter Road, roughly parallel to Montana Highway 1. Map programs may try to lead you southeast of Anaconda.

CONTACT 406-287-3541 or stateparks.mt.gov/anaconda-smoke-stack

DESCRIPTION
& HISTORY

One may stop for the view of the famed smelter stack, but the education on what the stack means is what's really outstanding at Anaconda Stack State Park.

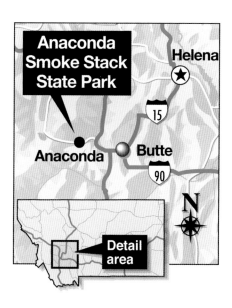

The interpretive area has a brick ring to show visitors how big around the stack is, as well as sculptures and informational signs on copper mining and smelting, the workers who built Anaconda and the role of copper king Marcus Daly.

The state park includes 10 acres at the actual stack, but the accessible part is 2.22 acres on the edge of Anaconda at the interpretive area.

Some facts gleaned from the state park:

- The Anaconda Copper Co.'s stack is one of the tallest free-standing brick structures in the world.
- The Washington Monument in Washington, D.C., is 555 feet tall; the stack is 585 feet tall.
- The inside diameter of the stack is 75 feet at the bottom and 60 feet at the top.
- The stack, on the National Register of Historic Places, was built in 1919. The smelter closed in 1980.
- The first Washoe smelter stack was 285 feet high.
- The 30-foot octagonal base for the "Big Stack" was made from 20,891 sacks of cement, 50 railroad cars of sand and 118 railroad cars of crushed rock.
- The stack is made from just under 2.5 million locally made tile bricks, the equivalent of 6.76 million ordinary bricks.

DON'T MISS

Walk around the brick ring that shows the diameter of the smoke stack. It paints a nice picture of how big the stack would be up close.

- The mortar that held all those bricks together required 41,350 sacks of cement, 3,850 tons of sand and 37 railroad cars of fire clay.
- The role of the smelter stack was to act as a chimney carrying off smoke and gases produced as byproducts of copper smelting.
- After processing in Anaconda, chunks of copper were shipped to Great Falls, where remaining impurities and metals such as gold and silver were removed.
- Copper magnate and Irish immigrant Marcus Daly promoted Anaconda as Montana's state capital and built the Montana Hotel in anticipation of housing legislators.
- Daly chose the site for Anaconda because it was near Butte with a natural water source sufficient for large-scale ore processing.
- During the early years of World War II, the United States suffered a severe labor shortage, and women stepped in to alleviate it. The Mill and Smelterman's Union resisted the idea of women holding smelting jobs, but as the U.S. Employment Service began to arrange importing foreign workers, employing women became more palatable. More than 70 women went to work at the smelter.
- The railroad connecting the Butte mines and Anaconda smelter was the first in the country to be electrified. It carried about 1,000 commuters per day in 1917, along with tons of industrial products.

Anaconda Smoke Stack State Park shows how big the smoke stack is (with an inside diameter at the top of 60 feet) and offers a view.

The Hotel Meade is the crown jewel of Bannack Ghost Town and said to be haunted.

27 BANNACK

"One of the best-preserved ghost towns in the west."

DESCRIPTION Montana's first territorial capital is a well-preserved ghost town rich with more than 150 years of stories.

ACTIVITIES Bicycling, bird/wildlife watching, fishing, history, ice skating, picnicking

CAMPING 28 sites, plus a teepee for rent. Reservations can be made at stateparks. mt.gov.

SIZE 1,529 acres

SEASON Open all year, from 8 a.m. to 5 p.m. from fall to spring, and 8 a.m. to 9 p.m. in the summer.

NEAREST TOWN Dillon

FACILITIES AND SERVICES Grills/fire rings, gift shop, picnic shelter, flush and vault toilets, tours, wedding facilities

DIRECTIONS Bannack is 20 miles west of Dillon. From Dillon, take Interstate 15 south for 2.5 miles. Take exit 59 for Montana Highway 278 toward Jackson/Wisom for 15 miles. Turn onto Bannack Road.

CONTACT 406-834-3413 or stateparks. mt.gov/bannack

DESCRIPTION
& HISTORY

Confederate and Union deserters alike, gamblers, outlaws, miners and businessmen poured into Bannack after the discovery of gold in Grasshopper Creek in July 1862.

By spring 1863, more than 3,000 men shared an increasingly lawless town. Another thousand lived up and down what Lewis and Clark already had named Willard's Creek, though that name didn't stick.

"Bannack would have been hitting its peak population. The gold deposit wasn't enough to sustain that many people," said John Phillips, Bannack State Park interpretive ranger.

A letter by Emily Meredith in April 1863 described a Main Street unsafe to cross, with bullets whizzing around and no one thinking to punish someone for shooting another.

"I don't know how many deaths have occurred this winter, but that there have not been twice as many is entirely owing to the fact that drunken men do not shoot well," she wrote.

Butcher Hank Crawford was named the first sheriff of this wild town. He shot the infamous Henry Plummer, who soon managed to run him out of town and win the office himself.

About $500,000 in gold left Bannack in the first six months, with gold going for $18 an ounce. (At $1,600 an ounce today, that's about $44 million.) The average American made less than $1 a day, but Bannack miners could make $5 a day. Skilled workers could see income of $10 to $15 a day – and then forked over $1 for a pound of sugar or $100 for a 100-pound sack of flour if the winter was severe.

Bannack gold was excellent gold. While most gold is 80 to 95 percent pure, some of Bannack's was an astonishing 99.5 percent pure, as pure as refined gold.

DON'T MISS

The annual Bannack Days, held the third weekend of July, draws about 6,000 people, with concessions, historical re-enactments, horse-drawn rides and old-time music. During the event, the ghost town becomes a living history museum.

Women were few and most of them of "negligible virtue" in Bannack's early days. Children attended subscription school, if their parents could afford the tuition.

In 1882, Bannack had 3,000 people and 300 structures. Today, about a third of the buildings remain, but they're spectacular.

In May 1863, the gold rush in the vastly richer Alder Gulch began, and Virginia City soon eclipsed Bannack.

In 1954, Bannack became a state park, but only in the early 1970s did the last residents leave the town, with milling and about 100 years of mining sustaining the community for all those years.

"This is one of the best-preserved ghost towns in the West," said Dale Carlson, manager of Bannack State Park. "We don't want to commercialize it. People want a feel for what a ghost town is like. We're frozen in time here."

As he walked the nonauthentic but accessibility-friendly boardwalk,

Mason Lodge 3-7-77 still has meetings on the top floor, and the first floor, which once housed a school, looks like children have just stepped away from their schoolwork.

Carlson opened the doors to the drug store. Undergoing stabilization, the building reflects Bannack's approach to preservation. Braces hold up the building that had started to lean. New boards – milled not from a lumberyard – have replaced decayed pieces.

"We don't renovate. We don't modernize," he said. "But old buildings will not stay upright without stabilization."

The Hotel Meade is six inches off-plumb and had to be stabilized and restored – an expensive undertaking to save the crown jewel of the ghost town.

"You don't expect to see a brick building in a ghost town," Carlson said.

Built in 1875 for $14,000, the hotel was the first brick courthouse in Montana. After the Beaverhead County seat moved to Dillon, the courthouse became a hotel, which operated until the 1940s.

The windows are high, the staircase curves grandly and Dorothy Dunn, a girl who drowned, is said to haunt the place, appearing in her blue dress to some visitors.

The vault dates from the courthouse days. Women and children of the town were ready to take refuge there when they thought the Nez Perce were coming.

The cries of dying babies are reported at the Bessette House, which served as an infirmary in times of influenza, scarlet fever, diphtheria and whooping cough.

Gold pans, sluice boxes and ditches gave way to hydraulic mining and dredging. Hard-rock miners dug gold-veined quartz with picks and then dynamite.

"They tried it all here to get all the gold out they could," Carlson said.

A barber's chair sits in the saloon.

The Methodist Church on Main Street still hosts weddings and lectures.

Two jails, the one on the right being the first in what became Montana Territory, are tucked behind Main Street. Before, offenders were warned, banished or hanged because no one wanted to stand around guarding a prisoner when there was gold to be found. Prisoners were bound to metal rings in the jail floor. Through the barred window, visitors can gaze on the gallows.

Bannack buildings are empty, used for storage, housing period pieces or displaying oddities archaeologists have discovered in Bannack.

The Masonic Lodge and School House remain a time capsule of the 1870s. The Masons met, and still meet, on the top floor, where the original carpet, historically correct furniture and Masonic art are in place. On the first floor, students of the town's first public school gathered. For 70 years, the school was open.

Bannack is much the way it was when Montana was just a stripling of a state, but it's a ghost town with Wi-Fi, flush toilets (in the summer) and a visitor center (closed in winter) with a movie room and historical artifacts.

Bannack State Park is more than a ghost town. In the winter, a skate pond is a popular attraction, with skates available. Even in the olden days, skating was popular in Bannack, and weekends saw parties form around bonfires along the ice. In the summer, the campgrounds and hiking trails are popular.

"If you haven't been to Bannack yet, you're overdue," Carlson said.

On August 13, 1805, Capt. William Clark stood on this hill to look at the Beaverhead River and land ahead.

28 CLARK'S LOOKOUT

"He stood on that spot."

DESCRIPTION Clark's Lookout State Park marks a spot where Capt. William Clark stood during the Lewis and Clark expedition to survey his surroundings and document his location.

ACTIVITIES Hiking, picnicking, photography, history

CAMPING No camping

SIZE 8.2 acres

SEASON Open year round, 8 a.m. to dusk

NEAREST TOWN Dillon

FACILITIES AND SERVICES Vault toilets

DIRECTIONS Take Highway 91 north out of Dillon for about a mile and turn left onto Clark's Lookout Road.

CONTACT 406-834-3413 or stateparks. mt.gov/clarks-lookout

DESCRIPTION & HISTORY

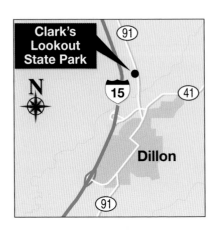

On Aug. 13, 1805, Capt. William Clark climbed an outcropping of limestone rocks to get a sense of his surroundings and document the location.

From his perch, Clark, who was a skilled mapmaker, looked through his telescope, made several readings and sketched a map of the region.

The spot where he stood is now Clark's Lookout State Park.

Park visitors have a chance to stand where Clark stood and take in the view he saw.

"He stood on that spot," park manager Dale Carlson said. "That's one of the documented places we can actually say he was."

Today, a large marble compass face, the design of which was taken from a small pocket compass that Clark carried on the expedition, is inlaid in the ground near the outcropping. The compass and the lookout are about a quarter-mile walk from the parking area.

The marble compass shows the three readings Clark took while standing on the lookout.

When Clark took those readings, the expedition already had reached the headwaters of the Missouri River. They chose to travel up the northernmost of the three rivers that created the headwaters – the Jefferson River.

"They were looking for a route to get to the Pacific Ocean," Carlson said.

Just as when Clark stood on the lookout, visitors today can see the Beaverhead River just below and can see the Tobacco Root Mountains, Pioneer Mountains and the Blacktail Mountains. Today visitors also get a view of Dillon.

In addition to the lookout, the park's 7.23 acres feature a nice hiking trail and interpretive signs explaining the navigational methods used by the expedition.

DON'T MISS

Take the short quarter-mile hike from the parking area to see the lookout where Clark surveyed his surroundings.

Beaverhead Rock was a landmark for Sacagawea as she guided the Lewis and Clark Expedition.

29 BEAVERHEAD ROCK

"It was a landmark for (Sacagawea)."

DESCRIPTION Beaverhead Rock is a natural rock formation that helped guide Sacagawea and the Lewis and Clark Expedition.

ACTIVITIES History, photography

CAMPING No camping

SIZE 30 acres

SEASON Open year-round

FACILITIES AND SERVICES None

NEAREST TOWN Dillon

DIRECTIONS Travel 14 miles south of Twin Bridges on Montana Highway 41. The pullout is on the west side of the road.

CONTACT 406-834-3413 or stateparks.mt.gov/beaverhead-rock

DESCRIPTION & HISTORY

"This hill she says her nation calls the beaver's head from a conceived resemblance of its figure to the head of that animal. She assures us that we shall either find her people on this river or on the river immediately west of its source; which from its present size cannot be very distant."
—Meriwether Lewis, Aug. 8, 1805

As Lewis and Clark traveled between what would become Twin Bridges and Dillon, their Shoshone guide Sacagawea spotted a distinctive rock formation. She knew she was nearing her relatives, from whom she had been kidnapped at about age 12 by a war party of Hidatsas.

"It was a landmark for her to know they were in the vicinity of her homeland," said Dale Carlson, manager of Beaverhead Rock State Park.

That gave the expedition hope that they would find Natives from whom they could acquire the horses they needed to cross the mountains on their way west. They had been watching for the limestone outcropping for days and were growing desperate. Winter was coming.

"The Indian woman recognized the point of a high plain to our right which she informed us was not very distant from the summer retreat of her nation on a river beyond the mountains which runs to the West," Lewis wrote.

And indeed, within a few days, the expedition came upon the Shoshone and their chief, Sacagawea's brother.

"It's a historical site, a national landmark," Carlson said.

A large draw for the park is that it's part of the Lewis and Clark Trail and referenced in their journals.

DON'T MISS

When you stop at the overlook to view Beaverhead Rock, take a look at the bronze sandhill crane sculptures there.

The significance of the rock isn't limited to Lewis and Clark and to the Shoshone, though.

The ancient trail past the rock became the route the ranchers used for the first cattle drives and then brought prospectors and settlers to Montana. A stage stop near the rock formation connected Bannack and Virginia City during the gold rush days when the road was the most heavily traveled in Montana. It operated from the 1860s to 1880s, and by 1920 most of the buildings were gone.

Wetlands of the Beaverhead Gateway Ranch now run near the base of the bluffs.

The Beaverhead Rock State Park is primitive, with no amenities.

The best way to see the spot about 14 miles south of Twin Bridges on Montana Highway 41 is to use a pullout overlooking the park. It has informational signs and a neat bird sculpture.

The approach to Beaverhead Rock State Park is easy to miss.

The park may be directly accessed, but the turnoff isn't marked and the road is rough. Call for more information about the access point at 406-834-3413 if you're feeling adventurous.

"There's nothing developed, but you can hike on rocks to overlook the valley," Carlson said.

One of the best ways to see the swimming-beaver shape of the formation is from the top of Clark's Lookout State Park in Dillon.

"Beaverhead Rock is only 30 acres, but it's a neat site," Carlson said.

Visitors explore the surprisingly colorful formations deep inside Lewis and Clark Caverns. MONTANA STATE PARKS PHOTO

30 LEWIS AND CLARK CAVERNS

"Fantastic!"

DESCRIPTION Lewis and Clark Caverns State Park is home to one of the largest known limestone caverns in the Northwest, filled with stalactites, stalagmites, columns and helictites.

ACTIVITIES Camping, fishing, hiking, wildlife viewing, photography, mountain biking, picnicking

CAMPING 40 campsites, a teepee and three cabins available to rent. Reservations can be made at stateparks.mt.gov

SIZE 3,015 acres

SEASON The park is open every day except Thanksgiving, Christmas and New Year's Day. Cavern tours are offered May 1-Sept. 30. Winter candlelight tours are offered several days in December.

FACILITIES AND SERVICES Camping, flush toilets, showers, RV hookups, water, picnic shelter, visitor center, gift shop, dog kennel in summer near the visitor center

NEAREST TOWN Whitehall

DIRECTIONS The park is located on Montana Highway 2 southeast of Whitehall. From Interstate 90, take exit 256 for Cardwell/Boulder. Head south on Montana 2 for about 8 miles. The park entrance is on the north side of the road.

CONTACT 406-287-3541 or stateparks.mt.gov/lewis-and-clark-caverns

DESCRIPTION
& HISTORY

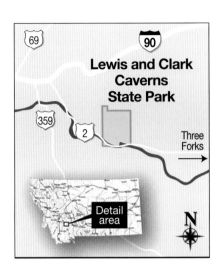

What Yellowstone is to the national parks system, the Lewis and Clark Caverns are to Montana's state parks – a crown jewel.

Among the more than 53,000 people who visited the park in the 2012 season, Mike Long from Los Angeles spotted the state park on a Montana map and worked a visit into his Yellowstone vacation in September.

"Fantastic," he said. "One of the things I found interesting is that you're not walking on one level, but the caves go down on many layers, and the further down you went, the damper it got."

Inside the caves, visitors are treated with sights of stalactites, stalagmites, columns and helictites as they work their way through the labyrinth. Many of the formations are named after food, like popcorn. Others are named for fantasy characters such as Snow White and the Seven Dwarfs. The Beaver Slide, a smooth chute visitors can slide down, is a highlight of the tour.

The two-mile, two-hour tour begins with a 300-foot vertical climb. The cave has 600 steps, mostly downhill, with bending and stooping required. Some passages challenge the claustrophobic or mobility-impaired, but tours include people of a variety of ages.

The campground is "very nice, better than expected," said Long, who camped there during his trip. In addition to 40 campsites, the campground offers cabin and teepee rentals.

The western portion of the park is open for hunting, and the Jefferson River may be fished all year.

In addition to the namesake caverns, the park offers about 10 miles of single-track trails that are popular

DON'T MISS

Be sure to plan enough time for a tour of the caverns. The tour takes about two hours and involves about two miles of hiking. The caverns are otherworldly inside and shouldn't be missed.

with hikers and mountain bikers.

The history of Montana's first state park also is interesting. President Theodore Roosevelt named the caverns for Lewis and Clark when he declared them a national monument. The explorers never visited the caverns, but they did set foot within the park boundaries.

The formations slowly formed, one mineral-rich drop of water at a time.

Stop to hear stories of the early cave explorers, the work of the New Deal-era Civilian Conservation Corps and the several ownership transfers before the state of Montana, which dedicated the caverns as the first state park in 1941. Lewis and Clark Caverns offers ranger programs throughout the summer months.

The park stays open year-round, but the caverns themselves are closed most of the winter. In December, special holiday candlelight tours are held. They require advance reservations and fill up quickly.

"It represents how the early explorers saw the cave, and it's a nice tie-in to the holidays, to see the cave by candlelight," said Lynette Kemp, park manager. "The formations are much different by candlelight. The whole room isn't lit up, and instead you get an intense view of the formations close by."

"It's a neat way to see the park, a quiet way," she added. "You'll walk up to the cave, and whatever the outdoor conditions, the temperature is the same. Most people visit in the summer and are used to the cave feeling cooler. This time, you feel the warmth of the cave."

No matter how hot or cold the weather is outside, the caverns stay a constant 48 degrees inside.

"Sometimes if it gets really cold, the caves breathe and you can see the steam coming out of the caves," Kemp said.

Visitors will find a visitor center near the caves and another near the entrance of the park. That facility has interpretive information about the caverns and park wildlife.

"People mainly see mule deer. If you're lucky, you might see elk or a coyote," Kemp said. "Mountain lions move through the park, and it's not unusual to see a bobcat."

Two buildings, Gillian Hall, left, and the Fraternity Hall, make up Elkhorn State Park, but they are just part of what's available for exploration in the ghost town and surrounding mountains.

31 ELKHORN

"Every ghost town enthusiast must see those two buildings."

DESCRIPTION Elkhorn is a silver mine boom town that is now mostly deserted.

ACTIVITIES Bicycling, hiking, history, photography

CAMPING No camping

SIZE Two adjacent buildings

SEASON Open year-round

NEAREST TOWN Boulder

FACILITIES AND SERVICES None

DIRECTIONS Elkhorn State Park is about an hour's drive from Boulder. Follow Montana Highway 69 southeast for 6.4 miles before turning left onto White Bridge Road. Take a slight right onto Lower Valley Road. Continue onto Elkhorn Road/National Forest Road 258. Most of the route is gravel and scenic.

CONTACT 406-495-3270 or stateparks. mt.gov/elkhorn

DESCRIPTION & HISTORY

Helena
284
12
287
Elkhorn State Park
15
● Boulder   **Townsend** ●
69   10 miles

In 1900, a far different scene would have greeted visitors to Elkhorn. Forty years after the discovery of gold there, Elkhorn had a fraternity hall, a stable, a train, a church, a school, a dozen saloons and about 950 residents.

Now, Elkhorn State Park, Montana's smallest state park, preserves just two buildings. They're surrounded by buildings old and new in a semi-ghost town.

The historic Fraternity Hall and Gillian Hall are picturesque reminders of that time. The heydays of Elkhorn were the 1880s to 1890s, though silver mining continued intermittently in the 20th century.

The Fraternity Hall Association incorporated in 1893 to build what would become the town's architectural and social center. Among the clubs using the upstairs hall were the Masons, Oddfellows and Knights of Pythias. Prize fights, plays, dances, graduations and more were held downstairs.

The neo-classical balcony is a unique touch, and its false front was common in mining towns of the era. Both buildings are empty.

"Every ghost town enthusiast simply must see these two buildings," Philip Varney wrote in his definitive guide, "Ghost Towns of the Mountain West."

The Elkhorn Mine yielded $14 million of silver and drew a population of more than 2,500 residents at its peak. In two months, the town lost 75 percent of its population after the Silver Crash of 1893.

John Bonan lives across the street from the state park in a cabin his grandfather built in 1892.

"Those two buildings have got to be the most photographed in any ghost town in the West, and it's been that way since the 1960s," he said. "There isn't hardly any in that good of shape" unless rebuilt or commercialized.

DON'T MISS

Neighbor John Bonan recommends following the main road through town and up the hill to the cemetery, which sits outside the state park boundaries. The three-quarter-mile gravel road is rough but navigable.

In the cemetery, you can see the headstone of Swiss miner Peter Wys (1824-1872), who discovered the silver veins of Elkhorn Mine. A visitor also will find the sad evidence of diphtheria epidemics the hit the children of the town especially hard from 1884-1889.

The Boulder Batholith is rich in minerals, which drew miners in the 1870s-80s.

A few times in its history, no one has lived in Elkhorn. Now, three full-time residents and some seasonal ones call it home. Most of the newer homes belong to descendants of the original settlers, Bonan said.

"It's kind of unique, like a resurgence," he said.

While the state park only includes two buildings, signs mark where others once were and identify some that remain standing.

The park is open year-round, with mountain biking, hiking and winter sports opportunities available in the area.

"A lot of hikers, snowmobilers and cross-country skiers come here," Bonan said.

Pass through the state park to see the cemetery, a good window into life and death in the boom town.

One can envision lively meetings held long ago in the Fraternal Hall in Elkhorn State Park.

Spring Meadow State Park in Helena is popular among birdwatchers.

32 SPRING MEADOW LAKE

"It's a nice family place."

DESCRIPTION Spring Meadow Lake is a 25-acre lake just outside Helena, offering swimming, hiking and fishing.

ACTIVITIES Hiking, swimming, picnicking, fishing, bird/wildlife watching

CAMPING No camping

SIZE 60 acres

SEASON Open year-round, sunrise to sunset

FACILITIES AND SERVICES Flush toilets, water, picnic shelter

NEAREST TOWN Helena

DIRECTIONS The park is on the west side of Helena at 2715 Country Club Ave. Take the Cedar Street Exit from Interstate 15 and follow the business loop into town. Turn right on West Lyndale Avenue and continue on Euclid Avenue. Turn right onto Joslyn Street and take the second left onto Country Club Avenue.

CONTACT 406-495-3270 or stateparks. mt.gov/spring-meadow-lake

DESCRIPTION
& HISTORY

Spring Meadow Lake State Park in Helena is an oasis of nature in an urban landscape.

Those who walk the 0.8-mile loop around the lake at the heart of the park might hear the faint sound of a train and a bit of traffic. But more so, they hear birds and rustling trees.

In the quiet of one morning, birdwatchers looked through spotting scopes on a pier, a couple of walkers passed through brush and a young family fished in the clear water.

"It's a good place to bring the family," Carla Sappenfield said. "We fish and swim. The kids always enjoy it."

Lori Chase, who lives nearby, walks the park's loop about every morning for "the scenery and calmness."

"It's clean and well-kept," she said. "It's a nice family place. You don't have to travel anywhere to enjoy a picnic and the outdoors."

She sees bunnies and birds and deer every once in a while. The signs warn people about handling turtles, but Chase hasn't seen any.

"I pay attention to the wildlife. I'm a gawker and a walker," she said.

She loves the quiet, and the park is a good backdrop for photos, too.

"Whenever I have visitors, they always want to walk around Spring Meadow," she said.

Allen Levens, also of Helena, comes to the park weekly in the summer.

"The lake and the trail" are his favorites.

"A lot of people come out to look at birds," he said. "I've seen turtles a few times, but they generally stay hidden."

No pets are allowed April 15 through Oct. 15. A gazebo is available.

In winter, ice skating is an option for visitors when conditions are right.

DON'T MISS

Enjoy the 0.8-mile loop around the lake. You'll probably see some birds, and if you're lucky, you might see some deer or a turtle.

Black Sandy State Park is upriver from Hauser Dam on the Missouri River.

33 BLACK SANDY

"An easy drive and great camping facilities."

DESCRIPTION Black Sandy State Park offers a shore to play on and access to Hauser Reservoir.

ACTIVITIES Boating, fishing, ice fishing, hiking, picnicking, swimming, water skiing, wildlife viewing

CAMPING 29 campsites. RV/trailer length limit is 35 feet. Reservations are available at stateparks.mt.gov.

SIZE 43 acres

SEASON Open year-round, with limited facilities Oct. 1-May 1.

NEAREST TOWN Helena

FACILITIES AND SERVICES Boat launch, fire pits, flush and vault toilets, RV dump station

DIRECTIONS From Interstate 15 seven miles north of Helena, take Exit 200 at Lincoln Road. Take County Road 453 for 5.1 miles. Turn left onto Hauser Dam Road and follow for 2.6 miles.

CONTACT 406-495-3270 or stateparks. mt.gov/black-sandy.

DESCRIPTION & HISTORY

A Saturday in Black Sandy State Park meant boating, fishing, playing and relaxing for the Wiseman family.

"My boy caught his first trout, and the other two kids like swimming," said Kris Wiseman of Helena as his son, Landon, 8, floated in an inner tube in a shady spot along the shore.

Wiseman said the park is an easy drive and has great camping facilities, where his parents spent the previous two weeks, with the rest of the family joining after school and on weekends.

His daughter Rylee, 9, played with a rope swing and said the park is "pretty cool."

"I like the view," she said.

Children ride bicycles and 4-wheelers through the park. Boaters and tubers make the most of weekends at the extremely popular state park just upriver from Hauser Dam.

This site is 43 acres. Electrical hookups are available May 1 through Oct. 1, but the park is open year-round. More than 50,000 people come to Black Sandy annually.

The park is an easy, scenic drive from Helena, and most of the route is paved.

DON'T MISS

Look for black sand along the shore of the swimming area toward the north end of the park.

Camping is available year-round at Black Sandy. MONTANA STATE PARKS PHOTO

The headwaters of the Missouri River are rich in history and natural beauty.

YELLOWSTONE
COUNTRY

MISSOURI HEADWATERS

MADISON BUFFALO JUMP

GREYCLIFF PRAIRIE DOG TOWN

COONEY

Shortly after the Gallatin River joins the nascent Missouri River, it passes a state park boat dock and limestone cliffs.

34 MISSOURI HEADWATERS

"Lewis described the place as beautiful."

DESCRIPTION Missouri Headwaters State Park marks the spot where the Madison, Gallatin and Jefferson rivers come together to form the Missouri River.

ACTIVITIES Camping, boating, bird watching, fishing, hiking, picnicking

CAMPING 17 campsites and teepee rentals. Reservations can be made at stateparks.mt.gov.

SIZE 532 acres

SEASON Open year-round

FACILITIES AND SERVICES Flush toilets, boat launch, picnic shelter, water, visitor center

NEAREST TOWN Three Forks

DIRECTIONS On Interstate 90, take exit 278 for Montana Highway 2 and Three Forks. At the end of the off ramp, turn left onto the I-90 Frontage Road. (Look for signs for the state park). Continue to follow I-90 Frontage Road for about 2 miles. Turn left onto Trident Road and follow it about a mile to the park.

CONTACT 406-285-3610 or stateparks. mt.gov/missouri-headwaters

DESCRIPTION
& HISTORY

The Missouri River is born in a beautiful place, a broad valley of golden grasses surrounded by mountains and ridged by limestone formations. It's a land of legends.

"Missouri Headwaters State Park is both the landscape and the layers of stories upon that land," said Park Ranger Anne Ore as she walked through a thicket full of songbirds on her way to the main event, the dawn of the mighty Missouri.

Home to pictographs, hiking trails, bike paths, camping spots and historical ruins, the park also has moose, deer and many different kinds of birds, thanks to the varied terrain within the 532-acre park. Riparian, arid and prairie landscape converge as the waters of the Madison, Jefferson and Gallatin rivers do.

On July 27, 1805, William Clark and four members of the Corps of Discovery reached the Headwaters as they scouted for Shoshone Indians, from whom they hoped to buy horses. He left a note at the confluence for Meriwether Lewis, for whom nearby Lewis Rock is named.

DON'T MISS

Take a quick hike to the lookout on Fort Rock. Enjoy the view and then continue along the trail to see the pictographs, for an interesting half-hour hike.

Fort Rock in the Missouri Headwaters State Park offers numerous hiking trails, amazing views and pictographs.

"Lewis described the place as beautiful," Ore said.

The crew enjoyed the abundant game but suffered from the abundance of mosquitoes. And before Lewis and Clark pressed on, they named the rivers for the president (Jefferson), the secretary of state (Madison) and the treasury secretary (Gallatin). The explorers had reached the headwaters of Missouri River 2,300 miles from the confluence of the Missouri and Mississippi rivers.

"Of course, these rivers had names before Lewis and Clark got here," Ore said.

The Gallatin was the Cherry/Berry River, the Madison was the Straight River, and Indians called the Jefferson Crooked River.

The rich resources of the region drew the Flathead, Bannock and Shoshone Indians, then trappers and settlers. As a child, Sacagawea was captured nearby. John Colter left the expedition early to return to the Headwaters. On one of those visits, he made his infamous run, escaping Blackfeet naked and fleeing on foot for days. Father Pierre Jean DeSmet celebrated Montana's first Mass near the Headwaters. Gallatin City twice tried to establish itself as a town at the confluence.

Lewis and Clark camped for three days at the Headwaters. You can, too. The park includes a primitive camping area.

Stop in the small visitor center for park maps, the summer speakers schedule or to chat with a ranger. The Madison and Jefferson merge beyond that, followed by the entry of the Gallatin on the other side of Fork Rock, a monolith with a few faint pictographs and striking views.

"It's a wonderful park," Ore said.

A fall visit to Missouri Headwaters State Park included a short hike to see pictographs for this woman and dog.

Madison Buffalo Jump State Park offers easy and more challenging hiking paths.

35 MADISON BUFFALO JUMP

"It's a great place for solitude."

DESCRIPTION Madison Buffalo Jump State Park is the site of a buffalo jump used by Native Americans for some 2,000 years.

ACTIVITIES Bird/wildlife watching, exhibit, history, hiking, picnicking

CAMPING No

SIZE 638 acres

SEASON Open year-round

NEAREST TOWN Logan

FACILITIES AND SERVICES Picnic shelter, interpretive display, vault toilets

DIRECTIONS Exit Interstate 90 at Logan and follow Madison Buffalo Jump Road to the state park.

CONTACT 406-285-3610 or stateparks. mt.gov/madison-buffalo-jump

DESCRIPTION & HISTORY

On a dirt road in the Madison River valley, a limestone cliff draws visitors to Madison Buffalo Jump State Park with its vistas and archeological treasures.

The cliff was used as recently as 200 years ago by tribes stampeding buffalo off the semicircular cliff. The arrival of horses left the jump largely abandoned.

An interpretive gazebo at the park explains how Natives used the jump, and visitors may hike where teepees once were erected and buffalo butchered.

A small picnic area is available in close proximity to the parking lot.

"Most people hike the trails," said Dave Andrus, park manager. "Some people go out there for a picnic. A lot of people like to walk to the interpretive pavilion. It's a great place for solitude, a walk by yourself."

The state park gets about 3,800 visitors a year who share four miles of hiking trail.

Those who make it to the top of the cliff have a great view of the Tobacco Root Mountains.

"If you want to hike up on the jump, there are teepee rings you can find and eagle pits, which are where runners would hide to allow the buffalo to pass before they jumped out to stampede them," Andrus said.

In the summer, the park is a great stop on the way to floating or fishing on the Madison River. The nearby Missouri Headwaters State Park at Three Forks is open all year, too.

In the winter, snow is sparse, so the hiking continues. Bird and deer hunters also come with the cold. Norris Hot Springs is nearby.

The park, which is on the National Register of Historic Sites, was not extensively mined for fertilizer as many other sites were. Neither has it been extensively surveyed by archeologists.

"A lot remains to be studied," Andrus said.

DON'T MISS

Displays in the gazebo up the hill toward the jump help explain the site.

Greycliff State Park offers an opportunity to observe a prairie dog community in its natural environment. MONTANA STATE PARKS PHOTO

36 GREYCLIFF PRAIRIE DOG TOWN

"If the weather is nice, they'll be out."

DESCRIPTION A large prairie dog town just off Interstate 90 provides education and entertainment.

ACTIVITIES Picnicking, wildlife viewing

CAMPING No

SIZE 98 acres

SEASON Open year-round

NEAREST TOWN Greycliff

FACILITIES AND SERVICES Picnic shelter, interpretive display

DIRECTIONS From Big Timber, drive east 10 miles on Interstate 90 toward Billings. Take Exit 377 toward Greycliff. Turn left onto Greycliff Road. The park is to the south of the interstate.

CONTACT 406-445-2326 or stateparks. mt.gov/ greycliff-prairie-dog-town

DESCRIPTION & HISTORY

Whee-ooo! Yip! Yip!

The Greycliff Prairie Dog Town State Park is a lively place along Interstate 90 between Big Timber and Columbus. The 98-acre park is home to a colony of black-tailed prairie dogs, the most common of five species.

"It's surprising how talkative they are," said Terri Walters, former park manager. "They have at least 11 different calls."

From staccato nasal yips as danger approaches to the "whee-oo" of an all clear, the ground-dwelling squirrels have at least 11 calls.

Another interesting aspect of prairie dog life is the burrow.

"It's a surprise how deep they go and the system they have," Walters said. "It's pretty interesting."

Black-tailed prairie dogs typically dig 15 to 40 burrow entrances per acre, many more than other species. Each burrow has two entrances, which lead to a tunnel up to seven feet deep and 25 feet long. A listening chamber, toilet, dry chamber and regular chamber serve specific functions.

The prairie dogs are more active on warmer winter days than colder ones, and cooler summer days compared with scorchers.

"People can take a drive in and know very quickly if they're out. When the weather is nice out, they'll be out," Walters said. "They use their burrows for shelter. They could be out any day of the year, unless it's really cold or really hot."

Within Greycliff's colony, an adult male, three females and their offspring make up a prairie dog coterie. Mating season is March, and in late spring competition for positions in coterie begins.

Ferruginous hawks, golden eagles, coyotes, foxes,

DON'T MISS

Drive the full loop of the park, and see signs explaining the structure of a burrow.

bobcats, snakes, weasels and badgers prey on the prairie dogs. And Edward Boehm of Livingston helped save them.

Boehm led the charge to preserve the colony as the Interstate Highway system was being built, with help from the Nature Conservancy, Montana Department of Highways and now Montana State Parks.

The prairie dog town is maybe 30 seconds off I-90. It has picnic tables (but don't share your lunch) and interpretive signs.

"It's a great place to have a picnic lunch and watch them run around," Walters said. "I'm pleasantly surprised how many people do stop. It's a nice opportunity and so convenient being adjacent to the highway."

Prairie dogs are surprisingly vocal, which is an entertaining experience for state park visitors. MONTANA STATE PARKS PHOTO

Only 40 minutes from Billings, Cooney Lake State Park is a popular water recreation spot. MONTANA STATE PARKS PHOTO

37 COONEY

"Beautiful how the prairie meets the mountains."

DESCRIPTION This reservoir near Billings is a popular water recreation area in south-central Montana.

ACTIVITIES Bicycling, bird/wildlife watching, boating, fishing, ice fishing, hiking, ice skating, picnicking, sailing, snowshoeing, swimming, water skiing, wind surfing

CAMPING Five campgrounds with 72 sites, 13 of which have electricity available. Reservations can be made at stateparks. mt.gov.

SIZE 309 acres

SEASON Open year-round

NEAREST TOWN Roberts

FACILITIES AND SERVICES Boat launch, camp host, dock, grills/fire rings, picnic tables, playground, shower, flush and vault toilets

DIRECTIONS From the Interstate 90 Exit 434 at Laurel, travel south on US Highway 212 for 22.5 miles to Cooney Dam Road. Follow for 8 miles to the lake.

CONTACT 406-445-2326 or stateparks. mt.gov/ cooney

DESCRIPTION
& HISTORY

More than 100,000 boaters, skiers and anglers come to Cooney State Park every year to enjoy the water and gorgeous scenery.

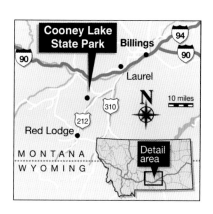

"Ice fishing is popular, and they're catching rainbow, ling and a few walleyes," said Jenny Alexander, park manager. "We had a few people come out and do kite skiing with the big parasails and ski across the lake ice."

The Beartooth Range provides a dramatic backdrop to the reservoir, a 309-acre site at 4,252 feet in elevation.

"It's beautiful how the prairie meets the mountains," Alexander said.

Reach the lake 25 miles south of Columbus on an asphalt and gravel route that takes about an hour to traverse. More visitors come from Billings through Boyd, a route that is completely paved.

DON'T MISS

Check out the dam at the east end of the reservoir. Make the most of the beach for a walk or a splash.

Being an easy, 40-minute drive south of Billings helps make Cooney Lake a popular recreation area in southcentral Montana, with 135,00 to 156,000 visitors a year, depending on summer weather. It's the third most popular state park, behind Giant Springs State Park in Great Falls and Lake Elmo State Park in Billings.

The electricity in the campground stays on year-round, but water is shut off in winter. Work is underway to expand the campground to include 20 more sites. Many will have electrical hook-ups, but some will be reserved for tent camping.

In the summer, the park has three boat ramps with docks and a fish-cleaning station.

Along the north shore, private homes overlook the lake.

While skating, cross-country skiing and ice fishing take over in the winter, the chance to waterski, tube and fish with their families draws people in the summer, Alexander said.

"My favorite thing to do at the lake is to go on my lunch cross-country skiing in the winter and checking on folks and visiting with them out on the lake in the summer," she said.

The cliffs of Sluice Boxes State Park turn red and yellow with fall foliage. Eagles often circle overhead.

CENTRAL
MONTANA

SMITH RIVER

TOWER ROCK

FIRST PEOPLES BUFFALO JUMP

GIANT SPRINGS

SLUICE BOXES

MARIAS RIVER

ACKLEY LAKE

Floaters near Sheep Wagon boat camp on the Smith River toward the end of a day of fishing.

38 SMITH RIVER

"What a unique vacation."

DESCRIPTION Steep canyon walls, a winding river, wildlife, pictographs and a rare multi-day floating experience await visitors to Smith River State Park.

ACTIVITIES Floating, fishing, hiking, swimming

CAMPING Tent camping only, 2-4 nights

SIZE 59-mile section of river

SEASON Float season is typically mid-April through mid-July, with some floating in Sep-tember and October, depending on weather and water flow

NEAREST TOWN White Sulphur Springs

FACILITIES AND SERVICES Grills/fire rings, vault toilets

DIRECTIONS Put-in location is at Camp Baker near White Sulphur Springs, with take-out at the Eden Bridge near Ulm.

CONTACT 406-454-5840 or stateparks. mt.gov/smith-river

DESCRIPTION
& HISTORY

For Matt Jewett, the best part of a float trip on the Smith River is launching the rafts at Camp Baker.

"That's when all the pressures lift," he said.

For the next five days, he will have nothing to do but fish and float, camp and chat. Cellphone service and Internet access are miles away. He's off the clock and on river time.

Jewett won't see a highway during the entire 59-mile float.

Floating the Smith River is one of the most prized outdoor experiences in Montana.

It's one of Tom Ware's most prized experiences, too. He's fished and floated the "majestic" river at least 25 times in the past 45 years.

"It's so different from your daily life," he said. "It's just so beautiful, and you catch a lot of fish, too."

His cousin, Herb Ware, has been snowed on, frozen, rained on for days straight, sunburned and bitten by bugs on the Smith.

"I keep coming back," he said as he neared the end of a trip. "It's my favorite place."

Permits are required to float the Smith, and they can be hard to come by. While prime floating is mid-May and June, permits are easier to get – and harder to use – in the shoulder season. Blizzards in April and low water in July have scuttled plans.

The majority of boat trips are three nights, with four the next most popular option. At minimum, the trip can be done in two nights, and four is the maximum.

Boat camp assignments are distributed first-come, first-pick for the 52 campsites in 27 boat camps. About 80 percent of the Smith River corridor passes through private land. The rest is a smattering of Fish, Wildlife and Parks land, DNRC school trust and BLM lands, and Helena and Lewis and Clark national forests.

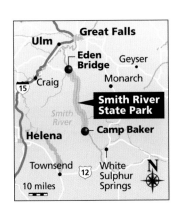

DON'T MISS

Take in the incredible reds, oranges and yellows of the Sunset Cliff at river mile 23.6.

Floaters must bring all the food, water and other supplies they need for the entire trip, with all trash packed out. Latrines are available at boat camps.

Twenty years ago, traffic on the river tended to be experienced anglers. These days, recreational floating is more common than it was. But, river rafting is much different than on a lake, park manager Colin Maas said.

"The Smith River is not whitewater, but it can be challenging," he said. "You need to have the skills to serpentine between boulders and rocks, to feather the oars and read the water, to know how the water will push you, pull you and spin you."

Less arduous than backpacking (as long as an experienced rower is at the oars), the Smith can be a great experience for children and older folks, too, Maas said.

In addition to floating the river, visitors to the Smith River also have the opportunity to view pictographs along the river.

"Scenery and fishing are the initial draw, with the social aspect of family, friends, camaraderie. People are thrilled to death, and what a unique vacation," he said. "The Smith River is a semi-wilderness experience. There are private homes along the river, but we're remote. You get a sense of wilderness. People like that it's primitive,

The last seven miles of the Smith River State Park float takes boaters through the prairie southeast of Ulm. Floating the Smith River is a tranquil Montana experience like no other.

and you have the cultural draw of the pictographs, too."

Special note: Permits to float the Smith River are awarded annually through a lottery system, with a $10 non-refundable application fee. Applications for the Smith River Permit lottery system are generally accepted from early January through late February, with permit awardees being notified in early March. Fewer than one in six applications is successful, with June dates the most coveted. Those who don't receive a permit through the lottery system can call the Smith River Reservation and Information Line to request any remaining launch dates or canceled permits. The reservation line can be reached at 406-454-5861 between 8 a.m. and noon, Monday through Friday. Hiring an approved outfitter is another option. For more information, visit stateparks.mt.gov/smith-river.

WHAT YOU DO FOR FUN
BY MAILE MELOY

When my brother and I first started going on the Smith River in the 1980s, when we were very young, we had rain gear made from black plastic garbage bags. When it rained—which it did—we sat huddled on a cooler on the raft, wearing orange horseshoe-shaped life preservers buckled over our bags. There were no permits or assigned campsites then, so there were groups jockeying for position and sending kayaks ahead to get dibs. You could get to a campsite, find it full, and have much farther to go (in your garbage bag, in the rain).

When the sun came out, shoulders blistered and sunglasses fell into the deepest swimming holes. When the wind came up, it yanked a tent out of the ground and rolled it away into the river. We made our aunt sing a funny love song she'd written, over and over until the adults screamed in protest. But those same adults told some really bad jokes and some long shaggy dog stories, and set the opposite bank of the river on fire one 4th of July—there was a frantic paddling across the river in the dark to put it out.

Tents are set up well away from the fire pit and associated food smells at Middle Ridgetop boat camp on the Smith River.

Our cousins' grandmother broke her ankle and had to be carried down from a hike, but still rode in the raft for two more days without complaining. There have been bears, lightning, hay fever, hypothermia, poison oak, and trips that made us swear we would never go again.

But mostly it's a mellow five-day float trip, with trout lurking under the banks. Panicky merganser ducklings flee the boats, their feet going like outboard motors, and the bald eagles perch overhead, unruffled. With assigned campsites, you know how long your day will be, and there's no unexpected slog to the

Givens Gulch on the Smith River marks a transition from the mountain canyon to a prairie ecosystem.

next free spot. There's time to hike up the canyon walls, overlooking the bends of the river, and to learn a kayak roll in a deep pool.

The group has changed over time, and you know someone's new boyfriend or girlfriend is a serious prospect if they're invited. The river isn't dangerous or technical, so you don't always learn what people are like in an emergency, or under pressure. But you do learn useful, everyday things. Are they cheerful after sleeping on the ground? Before the coffee is ready? Will they do dishes more than once? Can they share a two-man tent, and also entertain themselves? Do they know the words to songs? Those aren't the only criteria for choosing a mate or a friend, but they're not terrible ones. The test works in reverse, too: some people say, "This is what you do for fun?" And once is enough.

Maile Meloy is the author of the story collection *Half in Love* and the novel *Liars and Saints*, which was shortlisted for the 2005 Orange Prize. Meloy's stories have been published in *The New Yorker*, and she has received *The Paris Review's* Aga Khan Prize for Fiction, the PEN/Malamud Award, the Rosenthal Foundation Award, and a Guggenheim Fellowship. She lives in California and grew up in Helena, floating the Smith River many times throughout her life.

Smith River State Park covers a 59-mile stretch of the Smith River from Camp Baker near White Sulphur Springs to the Eden Bridge near Ulm. Mouth of Rock Creek boat camp is 8.9 miles downstream from Camp Baker. CHRISTOPHER CAUBLE PHOTO

Follow in the footsteps of the Lewis and Clark Expedition at Tower Rock State Park. Continue along the frontage road for a beautiful drive along the Missouri River.

39 TOWER ROCK

"A most pleasing view."

DESCRIPTION Tower Rock State Park is a chance to see an important spot along the Lewis and Clark trail while enjoying scenery.

ACTIVITIES Hiking, history, picnicking

CAMPING No camping

SIZE 140 acres

SEASON Open daily

NEAREST TOWN Cascade

DIRECTIONS From Cascade, travel 6.6 miles south on Interstate 15 to the Hardy Creek Exit. Turn right onto Old US Highway 91. Go around the trash collection area to the park behind.

CONTACT 406-866-2217or stateparks. mt.gov/tower-rock

DESCRIPTION
& HISTORY

The plains and mountains meet at Tower Rock State Park.

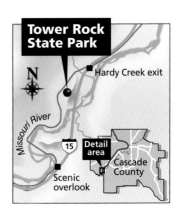

For today's visitors, it's a pretty walk and good views. For Lewis and Clark, who named Tower Rock, the landmark meant they were leaving the buffalo on which they depended and would have to find new sources of food in an unfamiliar landscape.

On July 16, 1805, Meriwether Lewis wrote, "at this place there is a large rock of 400 feet high which stands immediately in the gap which the Missouri makes on its passage from the mountains. It is insulated from the neighbouring mountains by a handsome little plain which surrounds its base on 3 sides and the Missouri washes its base on the other, leaving it on the Lard as it decends."

To climb the 424-foot rock Lewis called "the Tower" nearly to its summit meant "some difficulty," but the reward was "a most pleasing view."

That remains true, though one no longer sees the immense herds of buffalo the Corps of Discovery remarked upon.

Native Americans had a well-traveled route on the west side of the rock as part of the transcontinental Old North Trail.

The rocks are interesting – igneous chunks from the Adel Mountain volcano blasted skyward 68 million to 75 million years ago and then cemented together by volcanic ash.

One trail goes through the park. It's .25 miles and in good condition. Watch for rattlesnakes.

The state park has a gravel parking lot, an outhouse and informational signs. Only day use is permitted.

After your visit, continue through the canyon on the frontage road for gorgeous views of the Mighty Mo.

DON'T MISS

Watch for eagles circling above Tower Rock.

First Peoples Buffalo Jump offers a window into the culture and history of Northern Plains Indians.

40 FIRST PEOPLES BUFFALO JUMP

"One of the gems of our state park system."

DESCRIPTION First Peoples Buffalo Jump State Park is one of the largest buffalo jump sites in the country.

ACTIVITIES Hiking, bird watching, picnicking, heritage, history

CAMPING No camping

SIZE 2,000 acres

SEASON Open year-round. April 1-Sept. 30 the visitor center is open 8 a.m.-6 p.m. daily. Oct. 1-March 31 the visitor center is open 10 a.m.-4 p.m. Wednesday-Saturday and noon-4 p.m. on Sunday

NEAREST TOWN Ulm

FACILITIES AND SERVICES Flush toilets, water, visitors center, gift shop

DIRECTIONS From Great Falls, take Interstate 15 south. Take exit 270 for Ulm. Head north on Ulm Vaughn Road and then veer left onto Goetz Road, which leads to the park.

CONTACT 406-866-2217 or stateparks. mt.gov/first-peoples-buffalo-jump

DESCRIPTION
& HISTORY

For hundreds of years, Native Americans stampeded buffalo over the mile-long cliff, now known as First Peoples Buffalo Jump State Park.

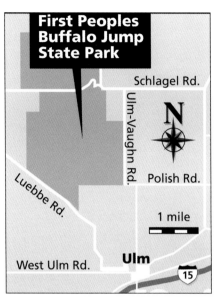

The buffalo jump located just outside Ulm is one of the most significant in the world, according to Roger Semler, assistant administrator for Montana State Parks.

"This park is well known in the cultural resource and archaeology community as one of the most prominent buffalo jumps in the world," he said.

The jump primarily was used about 1,000 years ago, according to Doug MacDonald, University of Montana professor and author of *Montana Before History*.

Like most buffalo jumps, First Peoples Buffalo Jump features a gathering basin, where bison would linger, and a cliff that the bison were stampeded over.

"They're not tremendously high," MacDonald said of the cliffs, explaining that if the bison fell too far, the meat would have turned to mush.

A trail leads visitors to the top of the buffalo jump, where, if they look carefully, they may be able to spot tepee rings, Semler said. They also can find remnants for the drive lines used to direct bison over the cliff.

At the jump's base, buffalo remains are 18 feet thick, although it can be hard to clearly make out skulls or other distinctive items in the remains.

On the top of the jump, visitors also can see a protected black-tailed prairie dog town.

A 6,000-square-foot visitors center near the jump's base helps explain the history of the jump, as well as other aspects of Native American history.

DON'T MISS

Follow the trail to the top of the buffalo jump, where you can look for teepee rings and drive lines. Look for buffalo remains at the base of the jump. Semler recommends hiking to the top at sunrise for a spectacular view of the Rocky Mountain Front.

The visitors center is designed to be hands-on, with a stuffed bison with a sign that says "Please touch," a tepee visitors can enter and displays where people can feel bison hide and sinew.

The jump is also a good place to spot wildlife.

"We have badgers, the occasional antelope, black-tailed prairie dogs, hawks and eagles, a lot of bird life and probably an occasional fox," Semler said.

Overall, the park represents an important part of Montana's heritage.

"I think it's just one of the gems of our state park system," Semler said.

Lester Oswald of Great Falls gives a demonstration of primitive bow shooting during the annual Montana Mammoth Hunt Atlatl competition.

A mounted bison is part of the educational display at the First Peoples Buffalo Jump State Park visitor center.

Fresh water flows from the spring at Giant Springs State Park. The spring is the largest in Montana.

41 GIANT SPRINGS

"Montana's most visited state park."

DESCRIPTION Giant Springs State Park is home to the largest spring in the state. It produces 156 million gallons of water per day, or enough to fill almost 240 Olympic-sized swimming pools. The park also offers miles of hiking trails.

ACTIVITIES Bird watching, fishing, hiking, picnicking, bicycling

CAMPING No camping

SIZE 4,000 acres

SEASON Open year-round, 8 a.m. to sunset

NEAREST TOWN Great Falls

FACILITIES AND SERVICES Flush toilets, water, picnic shelter

DIRECTIONS Giant Springs State Park is located in Great Falls at 4803 Giant Springs Road.

CONTACT 406-454-5858 or stateparks.mt.gov/giant-springs

DESCRIPTION
& HISTORY

Giant Springs State Park, located
along the Missouri River in Great
Falls, is Montana's most visited
state park, with nearly 300,000
people stopping in every year.

The focal point of the park is
its namesake crystal-clear springs.
Multiple bridges allow visitors to
look down on the water bubbling
up from the pool, as well as the
bright green vegetation growing in
the springs and the occasional fish
that finds its way there.

"This is a natural aquifer that surfaces here," former
park manager Steve Jones said.

The water that surfaces at Giant Springs comes from
the Madison Aquifer, originating deep under the Little
Belt Mountains.

While Giant Springs is the largest spring in the state,
it is not the largest in the country, said Matt Marcinek,
parks manager for Fish, Wildlife and Parks in central
Montana.

There are 18 major springs bubbling up into the
main Giant Springs pool. Several other springs are visible outside the pool and more are located at the bottom
of the Missouri River.

"This water stays pretty much at 56 degrees year-
round," Jones said.

That makes Giant Springs a beautiful place to visit
on a cold winter day, with steam rising off the unfrozen
pool and waterfowl flocking to it. It's also a nice place to
visit on hot summer days. The lush green park is often
20 degrees cooler than the rest of the city, thanks to the
shade and proximity to the water, Jones said.

The Roe River, which flows from the springs 201
feet to the Missouri River, was once named the world's

DON'T MISS

Watch the water
bubble up from the
park's namesake
spring. Then, go for
a hike. Giant Springs
State Park has trails
that extend for miles
on both sides of the
Missouri River.

shortest river by the Guinness Book of World Records, Marcinek said. However, since then Guinness stopped naming the shortest river, deciding it was too difficult to classify what is and isn't a river. Now the signs at the park identify the Roe as one of the shortest rivers in the world.

Lewis and Clark came across Giant Springs during their expedition in 1805, but long before that, Native Americans wintered in the area. Great Falls' founder Paris Gibson pushed to make Giant Springs into a park. The area was a city park until 1972, when the state park system took it over.

While the springs are what the park is best known for, Giant Springs State Park extends well beyond the lush green area surrounding the pool. The state park includes the picnic area across the road, and extends all the way west to Black Eagle Dam and east to Rainbow Dam. FWP manages another 3,000 acres of PPL land, putting the state park land and managed land at a total of about 4,000 acres.

A pelican wades in the Missouri River at Giant Springs State Park

Snowmelt from the Little Belt Mountains reemerges at Giant Springs about 25 years later. The state park is enjoyed in every season.

Sluice Boxes State Park offers hiking trails through a scenic canyon. Eagles often soar overhead. At the very least, stop at the scenic overlook along US Highway 89 above the park.

42 SLUICE BOXES

"A beautiful place to cool off."

DESCRIPTION Sluice Boxes State Park provides a place to hike near, float down, swim in and splash around Belt Creek as it leaves the Little Belt Mountains.

ACTIVITIES Bird/wildlife watching, fishing, hiking, history, hiking, picnicking, rafting, fishing, swimming

CAMPING Backcountry camping is allowed with a permit

SIZE 1,378 acres

SEASON Open year-round

NEAREST TOWN Belt

FACILITIES AND SERVICES Vault toilets

DIRECTIONS The park is 14 miles south of Belt. From the town, take Montana Highway 200/US Highway 89 south for 1.5 miles to the Armington Junction. US Highway 89 continues south toward Neihart. Continue for 9.6 miles to Evans Riceville Road. The park is on the left.

CONTACT 406-454-5840 or stateparks. mt.gov/sluice-boxes

DESCRIPTION
& HISTORY

In a shady stretch of Belt Creek in Sluice Boxes State Park, Booda Coles and Angel Schreiner stacked rocks into towers and dams.

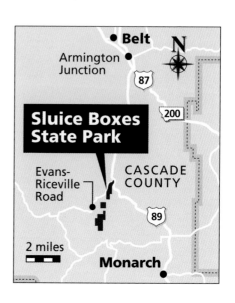

"It's a beautiful place to cool off, next to the water and playing with the rocks," Coles said.

They spent three to five days a week during the summer at the state park less than an hour from Great Falls.

"If it's over 90 degrees, we've been here," Coles said.

On a Sunday afternoon, they happened to meet up with friends – something that happened all summer – but they've also visited with people from all over the country and Canada as they played in the water.

"We've had an awesome, awesome time," Coles said.

They've seen floaters pass by, more when the water was two feet deeper than it was at the end of August. People jumped off a bridge in the park into the creek and hiked past on the seven-mile trek.

Plunked down on a shady beach next to crystal clear waters, Jeremy Wildhaber and his dog Beau ate lunch and crowed about a productive hike.

"We got about eight gallons of chokecherries in three hours," he said.

Wildhaber was driving to White Sulphur Springs when he pulled into the park to give Beau a rest.

Then he decided to return on the way home to Lewistown. And then he told a friend they needed to come the next day, too, and pick some chokecherries for syrup, fruit leather and whatever else they could come up with.

"So, I've been here three days in a row," Wildhaber said. "I guess I kinda like it."

DON'T MISS

Continue on US Highway 89 past the park for an overlook into the canyon.

After a few miles of hiking on the 7.5-mile trail, Robert Orser of Bozeman said the creek is the best draw for him to the park.

"I discovered it last year on a business trip and got lured in," he said. "It's a nice place. It's still in pretty good shape, not hammered from being over-loved."

The fishing is decent and the park is nice, minus the beer cans floaters leave behind.

Hiking, fishing, floating and en-joying fall leaves are just a few of the draws to Sluice Boxes State Park.

People interested in geology or Montana history should have the park down as a must-visit.

The park is along a former railroad spur, built around 1890. Trains de-livered mineral wealth from the val-ley to a Great Falls silver smelter, and the weekly "fish train" once chugged through the valley with fishermen, campers and partygoers.

Steep limestone cliffs flanking the parks are made up of seashells, depos-ited about 330 million years ago, when the area was under a vast sea. Tropical soil left the bright red Kibbey Shale before the land migrated north from the equator through continental drift and plate tectonics.

Angel Schreiner of Great Falls stacks rocks in Belt Creek at Sluice Boxes State Park.

As the Madison Limestone was lifted above sea level, ground water perco-lated through cracks and dissolved a network of tunnels and caves, many of which collapsed to create tilted strata, according to the state park.

The Madison Limestone became the largest artesian aquifer in the country, with some of the ground water that enters the formation in the Little Belts re-emerging some 25 years later 30 miles away at Giant Springs in Great Falls.

"I think this fountain the largest I ever beheld, extremely transparent and cold, very pure and pleasant," remarked Meriwether Lewis as the Corps of Dis-covery reached the springs in 1805 and tasted water from snowfall that melted around the time the British conquered Charleston, S.C., in the Revolutionary War.

This bend in the Marias River at the Marias River State Park and Wildlife Management Area near Shelby marks the halfway point for most floaters.

43 MARIAS RIVER

"It's like stepping back in time."

DESCRIPTION Marias River State Park offers access points to the Marias River, along with hiking and hunting.

ACTIVITIES Floating, camping, hunting, bird watching, fishing, hiking

CAMPING Backcountry camping

SIZE 7,360 acres, including the state park and Wildlife Management Area

SEASON Open April 1 to Jan. 15

NEAREST TOWN Shelby

FACILITIES AND SERVICES Vault toilet

DIRECTIONS From Interstate 15, Exit 358 east to Marias Valley Road, North 3.5 miles, turn west on Hjartarson Road, for 10.2 miles, then south 2.5 miles.

CONTACT 406-271-7033 or fwp.mt.gov/fishAndWildlife/wma

DESCRIPTION
& HISTORY

Walking through the Marias River State Park and Wildlife Management Area, it's easy to imagine Native Americans using the area as winter grounds or the Lewis and Clark expedition camping along the river banks.

"It's like stepping back in time," said Gary Olson, a retired Montana Fish, Wildlife and Parks wildlife biologist who helped develop the state park/wildlife management area. "It's pretty remote."

From certain areas inside the park/WMA boundaries, not a single man-made structure is visible.

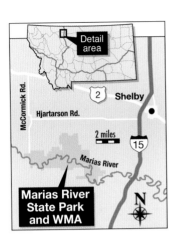

"'You don't even see the wind farm," said Olson of the farm that is located just over a rise from the river. "It's pretty wild country."

Montana Fish, Wildlife and Parks purchased the property, 5,485 acres of which is designated as WMA and 1,878 acres as state park, located southwest of Shelby in 2008 with the intent of creating a joint state park and wildlife management area that would offer areas managed for wildlife habitat with hunting opportunities, along with developed campgrounds, a visitors center and other facilities.

Plans for the state park also call for a river-accessed campground with two or three boat ramps, fire rings and toilets, but those developments are on hold for now.

"The boat camps could have been used for hunters or hikers," in addition to floaters, said Matt Marcinek, parks manager for FWP in central Montana.

The Marias River State Park and Wildlife Management Area is open April 1 to Jan. 15. Deer permits for the area are available via lottery, and the WMA is open for hunting of other species.

"There's tons of game in there," said Wayne Dagel of Billings who hunts there regularly with his brother, Clint Dagel, of Cut Bank.

DON'T MISS

Float the Marias River from Sullivan Bridge to Williamson Park. If you don't have two days to devote to that, visit the park and hike down to the river.

And the hunting there is different from many other areas.

"It is a very primitive hunt," Olson said. "It's pretty unique."

Even though Montana State Parks hasn't developed boat camps along the Marias, the river is still open to boaters.

Cottonwoods grow along the Marias River outside Shelby.

Floaters can camp within the park boundaries, although they have to pack out all their waste.

Mike Enk of Great Falls has canoed the Marias twice and looks forward to making the trip many more times in the future.

"It was a wonderful experience," he said. "You get a pretty good sense of what the river was like even when Lewis and Clark came through."

That section of the Marias is not dammed and mostly untouched by humans.

"This whole section is really wild," Marcinek said.

The float from the put-in at Sullivan Bridge to the take out at Williamson Park is about 31 miles. Only 13 of those miles are within the state park/ WMA boundary.

"Once you get into that wild area, you can just feel that sense of, wow humans haven't been here," Enk said. "It represents an unspoiled landscape that has basically remained that way since European colonization."

The float can easily be done in two days. On one of his trips, Enk spent three days, allowing for a one-day layover at camp.

"There are a lot of places to hike and climb around on the benches," he said.

Enk also has heard of people doing the trip in one day, but he suggests bringing supplies for an overnight stay just in case.

The Maris River State Park and Wildlife Management Area is a unique area, Olson said.

It will be harder and harder to find spots untouched by humans, and protecting those areas is important, he said.

"They just don't make any more of that stuff," he said. "If it's managed for the benefit of the public, I think it's a win-win."

Expect rainbow trout when fishing at Ackley Lake southwest of Hobson. MONTANA STATE PARKS PHOTO

 44 # ACKLEY LAKE

"Everyone can do their own thing."

DESCRIPTION Ackley Lake State Park offers camping, boating and swimming. The lake is stocked with rainbow trout, making it a great place to fish.

ACTIVITIES Camping, boating, bird watching, fishing, swimming, water skiing, picnicking

CAMPING 15 campsites

SIZE 160 acres

SEASON Open year-round

NEAREST TOWN Hobson

FACILITIES AND SERVICES Two boat launches, vault toilets, picnic shelter, grills and fire rings

DIRECTIONS Ackley Lake State Park is located about five miles southwest of Hobson. From Highway 87, turn south on 1st Avenue East in Hobson. Follow signs for the park.

CONTACT 406-454-5858 or stateparks. mt.gov/ackley-lake

DESCRIPTION & HISTORY

Summer or winter, the fishing at Ackley Lake State Park is usually excellent.

"There's a nice, healthy population of rainbow trout in there," said former park manager Steve Jones. "They're like footballs."

The lake is stocked, treating anglers to fish 10 to 15 inches long.

Ackley Lake is a popular ice fishing spot in the winter. In the summer, you'll also find anglers there, along with jet skis, swimmers and boats pulling tubers and waterskiers.

"It's big enough that everyone can do their own thing," Jones said.

Ed Althoff of Lewistown and Frank Siroky of Roy are regular fishermen at Ackley Lake. They've pulled plenty of good-sized trout out of the Lake.

"(Althoff) smokes them, and man they're delicious," Siroky said.

Ackley Lake became a state park in 1967. The water comes out of the Judith River and is stockpiled for irrigation use.

"It not only serves as recreation, but it also serves an agricultural purpose," Jones said.

The 160-acre park also offers camping.

The state park is most popular with people from nearby communities.

"The people in Lewistown and Hobson look at it as their own community park," Jones said.

DON'T MISS

Visit Ackley Lake State Park in the winter. You'll find a small village of anglers and ice houses established on the lake.

MISSOURI RIVER
COUNTRY

HELL CREEK

BRUSH LAKE

Hell Creek State Park has several walking trails through the Missouri Breaks.

The most remote state park, Hell Creek is along the Fort Peck Reservoir north of Jordan. A 108-mile drive – including 24 miles of gravel – separates Hell Creek State Park and Miles City, the nearest city with a population of more than 1,000 people. It's worth the drive.

45 HELL CREEK

"It's a nice state park. Come see it."

DESCRIPTION Hell Creek State Park is along the wild and rugged Missouri Breaks, with outdoor opportunities abounding. Numerous dinosaur fossils have been found there.

ACTIVITIES Boating, fishing, ice fishing, picnicking, swimming, water skiing, wildlife viewing, wind surfing

CAMPING 55 campsites, most with electrical hookups. Reservations are available at stateparks.mt.gov.

SIZE 337 acres

SEASON Open year-round. Office, showers, fish cleaning station and potable water available May 15 to Oct. 1.

NEAREST TOWN Jordan

FACILITIES AND SERVICES Boat launch, grills/fire rings, picnic shelter, playground, RV dump station, RV hookups, shower, flush and vault toilets

DIRECTIONS Head north on Jordan Avenue to Hell Creek Road. Follow for 24 miles to the park. The road is gravel, hilly and can be risky in wet or icy weather.

CONTACT 406-557-2362 or stateparks.mt.gov/hell-creek

DESCRIPTION
& HISTORY

The road to Hell Creek is long but scenic.

"It's a beautiful drive," said Brandon Swann of Helena as he worked on a four-point mule deer carcass at one of the many "man camps" in the Hell Creek State Park campground in the Missouri Breaks.

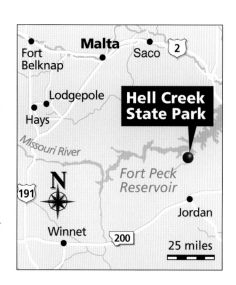

The park is 24 miles of winding, washboard gravel road north of Jordan off Fort Peck Reservoir.

Badland canyons, abundant wildlife and the twisting Hell Creek made the drive a pleasure. And then there's the destination: 337 acres along Fort Peck Reservoir.

"It's a beautiful place, great country," Swann said.

DON'T MISS

The Mule Deer Trail is a short hike but offers great views.

"I'd like to catch some fish out there," he added, gesturing to Hell Creek Bay where a lone boat circled.

When Hell Creek Bay freezes over, the fun continues. The state park is a popular ice fishing site.

Walleye is the big attraction, but Northern lake trout, small-mouth bass and "about every fish in this lake" have been pulled out of Hell Creek Bay, said Jerry Hensleigh, who works at the park.

Occasionally a paddlefish swims near the park, but the species isn't fished there, he said.

Swann's visit to the state park was to kick off hunting season with some buddies, a popular pastime at the park.

The campground is well maintained and has a nice playground, too.

Visitors should check road conditions before they go. The last stretch of road has a significant slope, though it's considered an all-weather gravel road.

"People come here all year. They come for a few hours and for two weeks," Hensleigh said. "There are a lot who come for overnight, too. I'd recommend three to five days at least if you're fishing."

The Lewis and Clark Expedition had its own troubles, none of which, of course, involved road conditions. Near where Hell Creek meets the Missouri River, the men nearly met calamity.

On May 14, 1805, they awoke to fog on the river, a rare occurrence. Later that day, a strong wind caught the sail and overturned their pirogue, dumping its contents into the river. Lewis wrote, "had the perogue been lost, I should have valued little."

William Clark wrote that nearly all the contents were saved with quick action.

Fishing and hunting are major draws to Hell Creek State Park. MONTANA STATE PARKS PHOTO

"This accident had like to cost us deerly; for in this perogue were embarked our papers, Instruments, books, medicine, a great proportion of our merchandize, and in short almost every article indispensably necessary to further the views, or insure the success of the enterprize in which, we are now launched to the distance of 2,200 miles."

The trouble didn't stop there. Soon after, six members of the expedition ended the day with a hair-raising grizzly bear encounter.

They shot at the bear, but he kept coming at them, forcing two men 20 feet off a cliff into the water. "So enraged was this anamal that he plunged into the river only a few feet behind the second man..." according to Lewis's journal.

When the crew finally killed the bear, they found eight balls had passed through him before he died.

Hensleigh focuses his shooting on antelope and elk, though people also hunt for mule and white-tailed deer.

One of the best ways to experience the Missouri Breaks is to launch from Hell Creek and tour the area from your boat.

"I really like it, but you better be prepared," Hensleigh said. "It can turn harsh, but people know what to expect if they've done research or been here before."

Hiking is another option in the park. Mule Deer Trail is a 1 1/2-mile loop within the Bearpaw Formation, made from sediments placed when a huge inland sea covered the area millions of years ago. PaleoTrail is three miles round trip into the Hell Creek Formation, which is known for its dinosaur fossils. It was a rich floodplain in the dinosaur era.

Tens of millions of years later, in 1902, Barnum Brown discovered the world's first Tyrannosaurus rex here and a few years later a nearly complete skeleton down to the 6-inch teeth.

"There's a lot of hiking to do here," Hensleigh said. "You could walk for miles."

Hensleigh, a Jordan native, has been coming to the park since he was a child, but he's seen other visitors surprised by what they've found in Hell Creek.

"It's the terrain and everything. They don't realize how pretty it is going to be when you drop down on the park. They don't realize what they're in for," he said. "The breaks are unique. It's a nice park; come see it."

The campground at Hell Creek is a launching point for fun on the water or the shore. MONTANA STATE PARKS PHOTO

Brush Lake State Park near the North Dakota border has a deep lake, sandy beaches and space for boating and swimming.

46 BRUSH LAKE

"A mile-long oasis of vivid blue."

DESCRIPTION Brush Lake State Park centers on a deep, clear lake surrounded by prairie.

ACTIVITIES Bird watching, boating, canoeing, hiking, picnicking, swimming

CAMPING 12 camp spots. Reservations are available at stateparks.mt.gov.

SIZE 280 acres

SEASON Open daily May 1 to Nov. 1.

NEAREST TOWN Dagmar

FACILITIES AND SERVICES Boat launch, fire pits

DIRECTIONS From Plentywood, drive south 14 miles on Montana Highway 16 to junction of County Road 258. Drive east 14 miles to Brush Lake Road, turn left and travel 1 mile to the park entrance.

CONTACT 406-483-5455 or stateparks. mt.gov/brush-lake.

DESCRIPTION
& HISTORY

More than 10,000 years ago, reced-
ing glaciers left behind a chunk of
ice the size of a shopping mall.

The spot where it melted is
now a crystal-clear lake with sandy
beaches. Just this side of North Dakota, Brush Lake State Park is the
only state park in the northeast
corner of Montana.

Created in 2005 as the 50th state
park, it takes in 280 acres along
Montana Highway 258, about 31
miles southeast of Plentywood.

Among golden stubble fields
and prairie, Brush Lake is a mile-
long, 60-foot-deep oasis of vivid blue. Visitors swim,
boat, water ski and watch wildlife.

The lake stays cool and fresh in the summer, and is
somewhat sheltered from the wind by the depression in
which it sits.

Brush Lake has been a gathering spot for Montanans for more than a hundred years. During Prohibition,
booze from Canada kept the Brush Lake Summer Re-
sort hopping, along with a lively dance hall. When "red
state" meant something else all together, the local Com-
munists held a major, national convention there.

Along the south shore, where the dance hall stood,
land remains in private hands. After the Roaring Twen-
ties, church and scout groups used the lake, though it
fell out of popularity in the years before becoming a
state park.

The park teems with bird life. Fish, however, don't
take to the mineral-rich, low-oxygen waters similar to
a hot springs.

Spruce from the forest that long ago surrounded the
lake has been detected at its bottom under thousands of
years of layers.

DON'T MISS

The Medicine Lake
National Wildlife
Refuge is just a few
miles southwest of
Brush Lake and also
worth a visit.

Woody Baxter, with Fish, Wildlife and Parks in Glasgow, came to the area to found a state parks program there and to establish a northeastern Montana state park.

A citizen search committee brainstormed 26 potential sites, visited 13 and presented four to officials, who backed Brush Lake as the first.

Brush Lake is an enticing picnic spot on the prairie. MONTANA STATE PARKS PHOTO

"It was wonderful" to finally get a park, Baxter said. "It was something the folks in northeast Montana deserve. We had 49 parks before Brush Lake and nothing in this whole area."

The park has two busy seasons, with temperatures accommodating picnickers, boaters and swimmers in force around Independence Day, and a second season centering around hunting season. Bird hunters camp at Brush Lake while seeking prey around FWP block management areas and the nearby Medicine Lake National Wildlife Refuge.

The well-developed campground has a dozen spots, with one handicap spot.

Closer to the water, a day-use area includes a boat ramp, dock and picnic area.

SOUTHEAST
MONTANA

CHIEF PLENTY COUPS

LAKE ELMO

PICTOGRAPH CAVE

YELLOWSTONE RIVER

ROSEBUD BATTLEFIELD

TONGUE RIVER RESERVOIR

PIROGUE ISLAND

MAKOSHIKA

MEDICINE ROCKS

The Tongue River Reservoir State Park draws many visitors from across the border from Wyoming.

A sweat lodge frame awaits use at Chief Plenty Coups State Park on the Crow Reservation.

47 CHIEF PLENTY COUPS

"He was really influential upon the Crow people."

DESCRIPTION Chief Plenty Coups State Park is the homestead of Chief Plenty Coups, a leader of the Crow Nation.

ACTIVITIES History, culture, hiking, fishing

CAMPING No camping

SIZE 195 acres

SEASON Open daily the third Friday in May through the third Sunday of September. Open every day the rest of the year, except Mondays and Tuesdays

FACILITIES AND SERVICES Flush toilets, water, picnic shelter, visitor center, gift shop

NEAREST TOWN Pryor

DIRECTIONS Take Blue Creek Road south out of Billings. After about 13 miles, turn south onto Pryor Road. Go about another 13 miles and look for signs for the park.

CONTACT 406-252-1289 or stateparks. mt.gov/chief-plenty-coups

DESCRIPTION
& HISTORY

Before settling into his home near present-day Pryor, Chief Plenty Coups had a vision of an old man sitting next to a cabin near a spring.

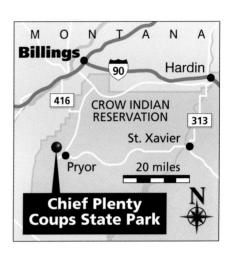

"He was seeing himself in old age," said Richard Took, ranger at Chief Plenty Coups State Park.

Chief Plenty Coups was the last traditional chief of the Crow Nation and is remembered for helping bridge the gap between traditional Native American culture and the white man's world during a time when Native Americans were being pressured to give up their old ways.

In 1884, Plenty Coups received an allotment of land through the Homestead Act. A spring, just like he saw in his vision, sat on the land, and Plenty Coups built his house nearby.

He raised fruits and vegetables and eventually opened a small store near his home. He encouraged his people to grow their own food.

He also encouraged them to assimilate into white culture, but also to keep their traditions alive.

"He always encouraged his people to get an education so they wouldn't be under the thumb of the white man," Took said.

Even as the Crow gave up their nomadic and traditional ways of life, they looked to Plenty Coups as a true leader.

"He was really influential upon the Crow people," Took said. "He packed a lot of weight with his words."

Plenty Coups was an accomplished statesman and ambassador. He knew several U.S. presidents and many foreign leaders.

In 1921, he represented all Indian nations at the

DON'T MISS

From the visitor center, wander down to Chief Plenty Coups' house. Be sure to visit the spring just outside his home.

burial of the unknown soldier at Arlington Cemetery. During the ceremony he placed his headdress and two coups sticks on the tomb to honor the fallen warriors. Those items are still on display at the Virginia cemetery.

Considered the Mount Vernon of the Crow Reservation, Chief Plenty Coups' home honors his leadership during a time of transition.

On a trip to Washington, D.C., Plenty Coup visited Mount Vernon, George Washington's estate. He was inspired by the idea of a national monument that was open to all people. When he died, he willed his own estate to become a place where all cultures could come together in a cooperative nature. His goal was not to glorify himself but to honor the Crow Nation and to bring people together in harmony.

The result was Chief Plenty Coups State Park, which features the chief's homestead, the nearby spring, Plenty Coup's grave and a visitor center.

The park, located near Pryor, about 40 miles south of Billings, is open year round.

During Plenty Coups' life, his homestead was often a meeting place for dignitaries and leaders.

"This was kind of like the Washington, D.C., of the Crow Nation," Took said. "He received all kinds of official dignitaries and visitors here."

While Plenty Coups worked hard to get along with the white man and encouraged his people to assimilate, it was clear that he wasn't happy about the situation. When interviewed toward the end of his life, Plenty Coups talked very little about the time after the buffalo were gone and many treaties had been broken.

"Most of his life story is told about the first half of his life," Took said.

Plenty Coups lived at the homestead until his death in 1932 at the approximate age of 84.

Today, visitors to Chief Plenty Coups State Park can wander through his house, visit the nearby spring and enjoy a 1/2-mile walking trail along Pryor Creek. The visitor center offers displays on Plenty Coups' life as well as many aspects of Crow culture.

Lake Elmo in Billings is one of the most popular state parks in Montana, with water to play in, a path to walk and a dog park. MONTANA STATE PARKS PHOTO

48 LAKE ELMO

"It's really popular for the water activity."

DESCRIPTION Lake Elmo State Park offers a 64-acre reservoir inside the city limits of Billings.

ACTIVITIES Swimming, fishing, boating, picnicking

CAMPING No camping

SIZE 123 acres

SEASON Open year-round, 5 a.m.-10 p.m.

NEAREST TOWN Billings

FACILITIES AND SERVICES Flush toilets, showers, boat launch, water, picnic shelter, playground, dog park

DIRECTIONS Lake Elmo State Park is located on the north side of Billings at 2300 Lake Elmo Drive.

CONTACT 406-247-2940 or stateparks. mt.gov/lake-elmo

DESCRIPTION & HISTORY

In the 1930s and '40s, Lake Elmo Supper Club, on the banks of Lake Elmo, drew crowds of people for dining, dancing and watching water skiers just out the club's back door.

"I guess it was quite a happening place," said Terri Walters, manager of Lake Elmo State Park, located on the north side of Billings, within the city limits.

Lake Elmo Supper Club is long gone – it burned to the ground in 1946 – but Lake Elmo remains a happening place.

Converted to a state park in 1983, the lake offers swimming, fishing, boating, picnicking and a dog park.

"It's really popular for the water activity and some of the land activity, too," Walters said.

Lake Elmo is the second most visited of Montana's 54 state parks, behind Giant Springs State Park in Great Falls.

Since Lake Elmo State Park is located right in Billings, it gets a lot of local day use.

Mona Blessing and Clarence Salley, Billings residents, are regulars at the park. They enjoy walking on the path that circles the lake.

"When it's nice, we can walk around the whole perimeter of the lake," Blessing said.

Even though Lake Elmo is located within Billings, it feels like it's out in the country, she said.

"It's always been nice to come here because it's far and away but not too far," Salley said.

Salley also enjoys bird and wildlife watching at the park.

"It attracts a lot of wildlife out here," Blessing said. "In the summer the kids are the wildlife."

DON'T MISS

Walk the 1.4-mile loop around the lake. You'll see the lake from every angle and maybe spot some birds and wildlife.

Lake Elmo State Park is a popular place to cool off on a hot summer day, but even on the busiest days, the lake doesn't feel too crowded, Walters said.

"You can swim anywhere in the lake that you want," she said. "That really spreads the recreationists out."

The lake is open to nonmotorized and electric-motor boats only.

Lake Elmo is stocked with fish regularly throughout the summer and is a popular fishing hole.

"We have a lot of trout," Walters said. "There have been some monster catfish that have been taken out of here."

The 123-acre park offers a 1.4-mile walking path around the lake.

"We're linked very closely with the trail system in the city," Walters said, making it easy for people to bike or run to the park and continue on the lake path.

Lake Elmo State Park also offers a dog park on the banks of the lake.

The 1.4-mile walking path around Lake Elmo is attractive whatever the season.

"It allows dogs to swim off leash," Walters said.

The lake itself, which was constructed in 1906, serves as the storage basin for the Billings Bench Water Association.

"It feeds the irrigation canals," she said.

The water comes from the Yellowstone River near Laurel and makes its way to the lake through canals.

"There's a lot of water that moves in and out, so it always keeps it fresh," Walters said.

The visitor center at Pictograph Cave State Park offers informational displays on pictographs, artifacts and other aspects of the park. Stop in the visitor center before exploring the park's three caves.

49 PICTOGRAPH CAVE

"The images change so dramatically."

DESCRIPTION Pictograph Cave State Park is the site of three sandstone caves, in one of which visitors can see pictographs. Some of the pictographs date back more than 2,000 years.

ACTIVITIES History, photography, hiking, picnicking, wildlife viewing

CAMPING No camping

SIZE 23 acres

SEASON Open daily April through September. Open Wednesday to Sunday October through March. Closed Thanksgiving, Dec. 24, 25, 31 and Jan. 1.

FACILITIES AND SERVICES Flush toilets, water, picnic shelter, visitor center, gift shop

NEAREST TOWN Billings

DIRECTIONS Pictograph Cave State Park is five miles south of Billings, about a 15-minute drive from downtown. Take the Metro/Lockwood Exit (No. 452) in Billings and travel south. Follow the signs to 3401 Colburn Road.

CONTACT 406-254-7342 or stateparks. mt.gov/beaverhead-rock

DESCRIPTION
& HISTORY

Symbols from more than 2,200 years ago and as recently as the 1800s can be found on the walls of Pictograph Cave.

In red and black, the more than 100 pictographs portray warriors, animals and rifles.

Billings

Pictograph Cave State Park

One of the easiest pictographs to decipher depicts seven rifles in a row. To the right, a pictograph made with the same pigment and the same diameter tool shows, what's believed to be, a beaver (flat tail, webbed feet) with lightning leaving its mouth and 23 dash marks painted next to it.

"The rifles' tips show they're being fired, being used in a skirmish," said Jarret Kostrba, Pictograph Cave State Park manager. "Back in the 1800s, there was beaver trapping here. What we think is this is about a fur trapping group."

In May 1823, the Jones-Immell group of the Missouri Fur Co., laden with a winter's worth of fur, was ambushed across the river from the caves by Blackfeet. Seven trappers were killed and the fur cache was seized.

"It's very possible the Blackfeet warriors came and painted this afterward," Kostrba said.

The pictographs are most visible during rain or snowmelt, which turns the sandstone translucent.

The Crow name for the cave translates to "place where there is spirit writing," which speaks to the way the images come and go, he said.

"This site is so unique," Kostrba said. "The conditions dictate what you see on a daily basis. Most of these images are veiled the majority of the time, but when we have snowmelt or rain, it percolates through the sandstone and the veil lifts. You can see closer to 30 to 40 pictographs instead of a half dozen on a normal day."

The site can look like it should be in a desert, with bleak, monochromatic sandstone. Or, it can look like a

DON'T MISS

Visit Pictograph Cave State Park on a rainy day or in the spring when the snow is melting. The moisture makes the pictographs easier to see. No matter what the weather, walk the loop to see all three caves.

rainforest, as waterfalls develop and pour over the rock overhangs and lush green grass and trees grow.

"The more you come out here, the more you see how this place can change with the seasons," Kostrba said. "It's the only place I know of where the images change so dramatically, too."

Pictograph Cave State Park actually has three caves (more like recesses beneath rock overhangs), all connected by a walking path, though pictographs are visible only in one.

Pictographs show seven rifles in a row firing, perhaps depicting fur traders.

Pictograph, Middle and Ghost caves provided shelter, beginning in prehistoric times. Natives following the herds along the Yellowstone River found protection from the elements, sweeping views of the countryside and a spring that sealed with an earthquake in the 1990s.

Wildlife sightings at the park include mountain lion, black bears, turkey, coyote, porcupine, red-tailed hawk, bald eagle, golden eagle, northern harrier, bobcat, mountain cottontails, rock dove, turkey vulture, mule deer, canyon wren, magpie, raven, crow and chickadee.

"This place is five miles from Billings, but we get so much wildlife up this corridor," Kostrba said.

One fall, Kostrba was in Ghost Cave when a bobcat passed within five feet of him.

"It's always a special thing when you have something like that happen," he said. "We're also a really good place to view hawks and other birds."

His favorite time is early in the morning when the sounds of birds echo across the park's natural amphitheater.

Midday, especially in the summer, more visitors share the park, but rangers are on hand to help people see the pictographs.

"Visitors, especially those who haven't seen pictographs before, have the idea they'll be vibrant, but these were painted thousands of years ago," Kostrba said. "Staff can point out with a laser pointer the fine-line charcoal drawings that aren't as visible."

At the base of the rock wall, the visitor center has a gift shop and informational displays. The restrooms are nice, too.

The 3,700-acre Yellowstone River Wildlife Management Area includes 200 acres designated for a state park but still undeveloped.

50 YELLOWSTONE RIVER

"There are some incredible back areas in there."

DESCRIPTION Yellowstone River State Park offers about 5.5 miles of Yellowstone River frontage, although the river is not accessible by car. This is an undeveloped park with no amenities or services.

ACTIVITIES Hiking, hunting

CAMPING No camping

SIZE The park is 200 acres, but is contiguous with the Yellowstone River Wildlife Management Area for a total of 3,700 acres.

SEASON Open year-round

FACILITIES AND SERVICES None

NEAREST TOWN Billings

DIRECTIONS Travel 28 miles east of Billings on Interstate 94, take the Pompeys Pillar exit 23. Turn northwest onto Highway 312 and follow it westward past Pompeys Pillar and turn north onto Bundy Road, cross the Yellowstone River and travel up the hill for less than a mile. Turn west onto Bozeman Trail and follow it for a little more than a mile to the entrance station.

CONTACT 406-247-2940 or fwp.mt.gov/fishAndWildlife/wma

DESCRIPTION
& HISTORY

Yellowstone River State Park is a great place to wander through the prairie and enjoy views of the Yellowstone River.

The park, near Billings, is managed jointly as a state park and Wildlife Management Area.

The 3,700-acre piece of land that makes up the Yellowstone River State Park and WMA was planned to be managed as a WMA with 200 acres on the east end making up the state park portion.

"We went a ways into the planning process," said Doug Habermann, Region 5 parks manager for Montana Fish, Wildlife and Parks. "We have a pretty well laid out plan for the park."

That plan includes a campground, but park managers ran into problems with the county requiring a subdivision plan for the campground.

The county also wanted to see some road improvements, Habermann said. All of that, as well as developing the campground, would be an expensive undertaking.

"It's kind of on hold at this point," Habermann said. "I don't anticipate it being developed in a long time."

Yellowstone River State Park offers plenty of exploring for an adventurous visitor.

"There are some incredible back areas in there, some really neat canyons," Habermann said.

While the river isn't accessible by car, it can be accessed on foot.

"People are certainly welcome to park and walk down the river," Habermann said.

The walk takes about 15 to 30 minutes depending on where people park.

The WMA and state park also offers access to eight sections of BLM land that previously did not have public access.

DON'T MISS

Get out of the car and explore this park by foot. You won't find designated trails, so wander to wherever looks interesting. You'll find views of the river from the cliffs above it, and then make your way down to the river.

Camping is not allowed on the state park or WMA, but people can camp on the BLM land. Visitors can drive within about 100 yards of the BLM land and walk the rest of the way to set up a camp.

So far, the main use of the park, purchased in 2008, has been hunting.

A two-track trail leads to spectacular bluffs overlooking the river valley.

The Yellowstone River isn't accessible by car but is just a short hike away.

Rosebud Battlefield is one of the most pristine of the Indian Wars, still drawing military strategists to study the events that transpired there.

51 ROSEBUD BATTLEFIELD

"There's a certain presence to the land that grabs you."

DESCRIPTION Rosebud Battlefield State Park is the site of one of the largest battles of the Indian Wars. Almost completely undeveloped, it's also one of the most pristine battlefields remaining in the United States.

ACTIVITIES Hiking, picnicking, history

CAMPING No camping

SIZE 3,052 acres

SEASON Open year-round

FACILITIES AND SERVICES Vault toilets, picnic shelter, interpretive displays

NEAREST TOWN Busby

DIRECTIONS From Billings, take Interstate 90 east. Take the exit for US Highway 212 east. Follow 212 for about 24 miles. Turn south onto country road 314. Drive about 20 miles. The turn for the park will be on the west side of the road.

CONTACT 406-757-2298 or stateparks. mt.gov/rosebud-battlefield

DESCRIPTION
& HISTORY

Each year some 300,000 people visit the Little Bighorn Battlefield National Monument, also known as the site of Custer's Last Stand. Fewer than 40 miles away, as the crow flies, sits another lesser known but important battle site of the Indian Wars.

Rosebud Battlefield State Park was the site of one of the largest battles of the Indian Wars.

Happening eight days before the Battle of the Little Bighorn, the Battle of Rosebud Creek on June 17, 1876, had major impacts on the outcome of Custer's Last Stand.

The battlefield is located off the beaten path and is less developed than the Little Bighorn Battlefield. In 2012, fewer than 5,500 people visited the site, but those who did were treated to a little-known, but fascinating history lesson.

"This has been kind of a hidden gem," said Bob Peterson, park manager.

Unlike Little Bighorn and other more well-known battlefields, Rosebud is almost completely undeveloped, making it one of the most unaltered battlefields remaining in the United States.

"It is as pristine in condition as it was in 1876," Peterson said.

The battlefield is used several times a year by the U.S. armed forces to study military strategy, particularly in an area where troops are taking on an enemy who is more familiar with the land.

"They look to see what happened here and critique what was done," he said.

The impetus for the battle of Rosebud Creek was the edict of 1875, saying that all Indian people needed to be on a reservation by the end of the year.

DON'T MISS

Drive the loop road that runs through the park. Stop at the vista point above a large gully and hike to the buffalo jump.

"If they weren't, then the U.S. armed forces would come after them," Peterson explained.

Lakota leaders Sitting Bull and Crazy Horse decided not to follow those orders, instead moving to the Powder River area, about 80 miles from Rosebud.

On their way from the Bighorn Battlefield near Crow Agency to Sheridan, Wyo., British couple Elizabeth and Ian Cunningham stopped at the Rosebud Battlefield State Park.

That was one of the last places where buffalo roamed freely. The leaders invited others to leave the reservations and join them to live the way Native Americans had always lived.

"The groups just kept getting bigger," Peterson said.

Eventually, Gen. Philip Sheridan, who was in Chicago, sent three columns of troops to force the Indians onto reservations.

Leading one of those columns was Gen. George Crook, based at Fort Fetterman, near present-day Douglas, Wyo. Crook and his troops, along with horses and pack mules, made their way to present-day Sheridan and arrived at what is now Rosebud Battlefield State Park around 8 a.m. on June 17, 1876, where they stopped for breakfast. Along the way, he picked up about 90 miners who joined the troops because they thought it would be fun to fight Indians.

"European white Americans wanted blood," Peterson said of the climate at that time. "Racism and bigotry just was rampant in the newspapers."

The same night that Crook and his men were riding to Rosebud Battlefield, Crazy Horse and his warriors also were making their way to the area.

"They rode here all night," Peterson said.

Each warrior was riding a horse and leading another horse.

"The horse they were leading was their war horse," he explained.

Some say there were more than 2,000 Native American warriors at the battle, others say the number was closer to 700.

Around 8:30 a.m., the battle erupted. It went on until about 2:30 in the afternoon.

Visitors to the park can see the ridges where the battle was fought and Crook's Hill, where Crook set up his command. Visitors also can see the spot where a female Cheyenne warrior rode into gun fire to save her brother.

At the end of that June day, the air was filled with black powder smoke and the screams of dying men and horses, Peterson said.

"People died here, both sides," Peterson said.

Nine U.S. soldiers died during the battle and about 40 were wounded. The remaining troops buried the causalities.

"We really don't know where the grave is," Peterson said.

Crook had all the men ride over it to hide it. Crazy Horse may have found it or the grave may still be intact somewhere.

"We don't have any real good estimate of how many Native Americans were killed or wounded," Peterson said.

After the battle, Crook took his men back to Sheridan so he could get reinforcements and supplies. The troops fired some 50,000 rounds of ammunition during the battle.

"Crook pulled out," Peterson said.

Eight days later when Lt. Col. George Armstrong Custer went to the Little Bighorn, Crook declined to join him, saying he still needed supplies and reinforcements.

Some blamed Crook for Custer's death, since he didn't support Custer in that battle.

"Crook took a lot of heat throughout his career," Peterson said.

Crook went on to capture Apache leader Geronimo, but never lived down the role he played in the Little Bighorn and Rosebud battles.

The battle of Rosebud Creek is significant because it marked the first time a large group of Indian warriors took on a large group of U.S. soldiers. Prior to that, battles of the Indian Wars had mainly been raids.

"This was actually mano y mano," Peterson said.

Crazy Horse found that the method worked and used it again at the battle of the Little Bighorn.

Today, a road makes a loop through part of the park, and visitors are welcome to wander through the fields. Those looking for a short hike can walk to the base of a buffalo jump that was used as far back as 8500 BC.

"There are petroglyphs that are etched in that wall of the buffalo jump," Peterson said.

Many visitors are drawn to the site for its historical significance, but others visit the park because it offers incredible scenery and quite solitude.

"There's a certain feeling to the land, there's a certain presence to the land that grabs you," Peterson said.

Tongue River Reservoir State Park on the southeastern Montana prairie has dramatic scenery. The park drew these Sheridan, Wyo., teenagers on a hot afternoon.

52 TONGUE RIVER RESERVOIR

"We offer fishing that isn't common elsewhere."

DESCRIPTION Tongue River Reservoir is 12 miles long and offers great fishing, camping and boating.

ACTIVITIES Camping, fishing, boating, swimming, water skiing, wind surfing

CAMPING More than 150 campsites, including 40 paved campsites with electrical hookups. Reservations can be made in advance at stateparks.mt.gov.

SIZE 30 acres

SEASON Open year-round

FACILITIES AND SERVICES Fish cleaning station, marina, concessions, boat launch, boat rental, LP gas refill, vault toilets, RV hookups, RV dump station

NEAREST TOWN Decker

Directions: From Billings, head east on Interstate 90. Travel across the Wyoming border and take Exit 16 for Wyoming-339 and Decker. Head north on Wyoming 338, which turns into Montana 314, and drive for about 20 miles to the park.

CONTACT 406-757-2298 or stateparks. mt.gov/tongue-river-reservoir

DESCRIPTION
& HISTORY

Stripes of red shale, juniper canyons, prairies and water combine for memorable scenery at Tongue River Reservoir State Park.

In coal country near the Wyoming border about two hours southeast of Billings, the state park hosts more than 50,000 visitors every year.

The park includes six miles of reservoir frontage and more than 150 campsites, the most campsites of any state park.

Until Montana replaced resident day-use fees with an optional license-plate fee, Tongue River Reservoir visitors were evenly split between Montana and Wyoming residents. Now, about 85 percent of visitors come from all over Montana.

Nonresidents pay a $5 day-use fee and more to camp.

"We offer fishing that isn't common elsewhere, walleye, bass, crappie and Northern pike," park manager Bob Peterson said. "Montana hammers trout fishing, and we see a lot at Tongue River who want to pursue walleye."

Crappies are the easiest to catch in the warm water fishery, and big crappie fries are common on the shore.

"Anyone can bring a kid to Tongue River Reservoir and make a fisherman of them," Peterson said. "They'll catch crappies until they're sick of them."

Kids also enjoy swimming at the park.

Sheridan teenager Chloe Scholtz enjoys visiting Tongue River Reservoir State Park on hot days to splash around the water.

"It's pretty here," Scholtz said. "We come to the cliffs and Sand Point campground."

In the winter, it's a popular place to ice fish.

DON'T MISS

Drive all the way along the reservoir to the dam. You'll be treated to some neat views of the dam and the water.

At certain times of the year, accessing Pirogue Island may involve wading through channels of the Yellowstone River. At times the water is too high to safely access the park.

53 PIROGUE ISLAND

"Walking and nature study are the most popular."

DESCRIPTION Pirogue Island, covered in cotton wood trees, sits in the Yellowstone River. It's a great place to hike and see wildlife.

ACTIVITIES Hiking, wildlife watching, picnicking, bird watching

CAMPING No camping

SIZE 269 acres

SEASON Open year-round, but water levels, especially in spring, can making crossing onto the island impossible.

NEAREST TOWN Miles City

FACILITIES AND SERVICES Vault toilets

DIRECTIONS Take Montana Highway 59 northwest out of Miles City toward the airport, following the signs to Montana Highway 489 to Pirogue Island Road. Map programs may try to direct visitors to the opposite banks of the Yellowstone.

CONTACT 406-495-3256 or stateparks. mt.gov/pirogue-island

DESCRIPTION
& HISTORY

Reaching the grasslands at the center of Pirogue Island State Park, at least one visitor has felt compelled to yell, ala "Lion King," "Baaaaa, sowenya, mamabeatsebabah!"

Though circled and dotted by cottonwoods, the island has a grassland at its center, home to mule and whitetail deer, fox, squirrels, bald eagles and waterfowl. Sodbusters once plowed fields on the islands.

The island also is home to more than 140 species of plants, the most prominent are the 65- to 100-foot-tall plains cottonwood. Visitors can see ice scars on the trunks of cottonwood trees caused by past floods. The peach-leaf willow, green ash and redosier dogwood are other trees on the island.

The park is 269 acres with 2.8 miles of level hiking trails. Interpretive signs offer interesting notes on the history and wildlife of the island.

"What a nice place for folks to get away once the water goes down," said Doug Habermann, regional parks manager.

"Walking and nature study are the most popular, and we get folks who just hang out in the parking lot," he added. "A few people mountain bike, and fishing for sure. People look for moss agates."

Habermann said the park averages 200 to 300 vehicles a month, with a couple people in each.

"The park is treasured by locals," he said.

Others stop by as they float down the river. Pirogue Island State Park is 500 miles from where the Yellowstone River begins and 170 miles from its end.

"There are people who have discovered the lower Yellowstone is a pretty nice place to float," Habermann said.

DON'T MISS

As long as water levels are safe, ford the channel of the Yellowstone to reach the island. Once there, walk the 2.8-mile loop around the island.

The island has a good representation of natural life along the Yellowstone, and in eastern Montana a huge amount of life centers along that river.

"It's a nice, natural setting with peace and quiet," he said. "Hopefully it's a place kids get a taste of nature and a chance to be in the outdoors."

Habermann has walked the park to wind down at the end of his day.

The park is not formally developed, and sometimes side channels flood, limiting or even cutting off access. Yet the wild nature of the island helps visitors imagine what the Corps of Discovery saw when William Clark led a party down the Yellowstone River and camped on an island near what became Miles City. It's hard to know exactly where they camped because the river channel changes, moving back and forth across the valley, Habermann said.

"You're looking across at stockyard and a lumber mill but you still get that feel," he said. "It's a wild island."

If the water is up in the channels, "people cross at their own risk," Habermann said.

Water levels are usually highest in the spring. It varies year to year how long the high, unsafe water lasts.

"I can't say when it becomes safe," Habermann said. "It's not too far to pack a canoe and paddle across."

Cottonwood trees show signs of flooding. The center of the island has a neat meadow, with a trail that circles the island.

Montana's biggest state park, Makoshika warrants a longer visit. Pay attention to the weather before venturing too far.

54 MAKOSHIKA

"This has been known as a dinosaur park, but it's so much more."

DESCRIPTION More than 10 species of dinosaurs have been discovered in Makoshika State Park and visitors will find unique rock formations there.

ACTIVITIES Camping, hiking, bird watching, mountain biking, picnicking

CAMPING 16 campsites. Reservations can be made at stateparks.mt.gov.

SIZE 11,538 acres

SEASON Open year-round

FACILITIES AND SERVICES Camping, flush toilets, water, visitor center, gift shop

NEAREST TOWN Glendive

DIRECTIONS Makoshika is located on the southeast side of Glendive at 1301 Snyder St.

CONTACT 406-377-6256 or stateparks. mt.gov/makoshika

DESCRIPTION
& HISTORY

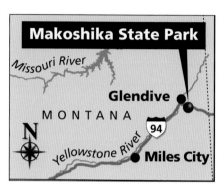

When Lily Soderlund heard "badlands," she didn't picture the scenic glory that awaited her in eastern Montana.

"The 'badlands,' it's completely different than I thought," she said. "Now I associate this place with the '90s version of bad, like it's so crazy/awesome out here."

The AmeriCorps volunteer from Ohio camped for a couple nights at the top of a ridge in Makoshika State Park with a 360-degree view of canyons, rock formations, deer, flowers and more.

About half the species of birds found in Montana can be seen in the park, as well as about half of the state's flower species.

More than 10 species of dinosaurs have also been discovered in Makoshika.

For millions of years of the Late Cretaceous Period – 100 to 66 million years ago – the sea level was much higher and what are now the great plains was a warm, shallow sea. As the Rocky Mountains thrust upward, sometimes Makoshika was under the water. Sometimes it wasn't.

The Bearpaw shale – the oldest exposed in the area – contains fossils of swimming reptiles such as the mosasaur, giant mollusks and other sea creatures.

The best-known fossil in Makoshika is a triceratops, but edmontosaurus and tyrannosaurus rex have also been found.

Makoshika is part of the Hell Creek Formation, where the youngest fossil in the world has been found, a 65-million-year-old triceratops Yale scientists call "the last known nonavian dinosaurs of the Cretaceous."

Finding a fossil takes a good eye and removing them is illegal. However, for a guaranteed fossil find, head to the visitors center at the park's entrance.

DON'T MISS

Give yourself lots of time to explore this huge park. While you're there go for a hike. Makoshika has many miles of trails. Try the 1.5-mile Cap Rock Nature Trail or the Kinney Coulee Trail. If you're really looking for a challenge, Makoshika holds a 10-kilometer race up its steep road during the annual Buzzard Day event each June.

Displays, which include rocks and fossils one may touch, take visitors through hundreds of millions of years of history in a few minutes. One of the best fossils on display is a triceratops skull.

Makoshika's history didn't end with the dinosaurs. The oldest Paleo-Indian artifacts found in the park date from 12,000 years ago.

"This has always been known as a dinosaur park, but it's so much more," said Doug Habermann, regional park manager.

A derivative of the Lakota term for bad land or land of bad spirits, "maco sica," Makoshika is pronounced "Mah-koh-shi-kah."

"This is such an antithesis of what western Montana is, yet it's beautiful," Soderlund said. "You can travel eight hours across the state, and it's still beautiful."

Glendive is adjacent to the park, so it is easy to visit.

"For locals, they come and relax," Habermann said. "Some families come every weekend."

Yet at the same time, the elbow room is extreme.

"Within your sight, there are no people," he said, gesturing across the park.

"It's wilderness right here. There's a huge potential for solitude," he said. "The landscape lends itself to feeling like no one has ever been there before. There are places in this park few, if any, people have even walked to."

Lily Soderlund watches the sun sink at Makoshika State Park. She found the badlands to be beautiful.

Makoshika is 18 square miles in size, but if the contour of the land is taken into account, it's more like 400 square miles.

"It's one of the jewels of the system, our largest park," he said. "We're privileged to have these wonderful places."

Hiking, biking, walking, backcountry camping, disc golf, interpretive talks and the views of badlands landscape occupy visitors in the summer. In winter, the park has cross-country skiing.

"In different seasons, you get different tones and colors," Habermann said. "It's beautiful and open year-round."

The park can be hot in the summer – Glendive has reached a state record 117 degrees – and exceptionally cold in the winter. The shoulder season, though, is exceptional, Habermann said.

A family donated much of the park, and local folks have embraced it since Makoshika became a state park in 1953.

Though he's traveled around the world, Jim Swanson, head of Friends of Makoshika, said he would rather be in the state park than anywhere else.

"Everywhere you turn it's different," he said. "You sit and just look at the beauty of it, every aspect of the park in various times of the day. If you let yourself go, it's the most comforting thing to listen to the quiet, the wind. It's so peaceful."

A dramatic storm lights up Makoshika State Park near Glendive. MONTANA STATE PARKS PHOTO.

Makoshika's rapid erosion means the state park is ever changing.

Fascinating sandstone formations dot the prairie at Medicine Rocks State Park north of Ekalaka.

55 MEDICINE ROCKS

"It's a photographer's playground."

DESCRIPTION Medicine Rocks State Park is covered in unique sandstone formations that rise out of the prairie.

ACTIVITIES Camping, hiking, photography, picnicking, wildlife viewing

CAMPING 12 campsites

SIZE 330 acres

SEASON Open year-round

NEAREST TOWN Ekalaka

FACILITIES AND SERVICES Vault toilets, water, picnic shelter

DIRECTIONS The park is located on Highway 7 about seven miles north of Ekalaka and 30 miles south of Baker.

CONTACT 406-377-6256 or stateparks.mt.gov/medicine-rocks

DESCRIPTION
& HISTORY

Traveling on Montana Highway 7 south from Baker toward Ekalaka, the road flows through rolling hills and sweeping prairies.

Then it rounds a corner and drops down a hill and suddenly large sandstone outcroppings come into view rising out of the prairie.

"I don't know of anything like it anywhere else," said Frank Mehling, who ranches nearby.

Those unique rock formations make up Medicine Rocks State Park, a 330-acre park located about six miles north of Ekalaka.

Mehling has seen other sandstone outcroppings located around cliffs or rims.

"These just kind of rise out of the plains," he said. "It's a neat area, there's no doubt about that."

The sandstone rocks form pillars, caves, archways and towers and have the pockmarked look of Swiss cheese because of millions of years of weathering. Between the outcroppings lie some areas of pine forest and other areas of open plains.

These unique rock formations were formed through a complex sequence of geological events. Some 60 million years ago, the northern Great Plains were covered by a huge island lake. The edges of the lake were swampy and forested with a slow-moving shallow river cutting through. That river carried sediment from the newly forming Rocky Mountains.

Some of those sediments were deposited along the river's path, creating sandbars. Over the eons, those sandbars were turned to sandstone through compaction. Wind, water and temperature extremes constantly took their toll on the rock. The more resistant materials stayed, while the softer materials gave way to erosion.

DON'T MISS

There's a well at the park entrance. Stop and fill a water bottle there. Some say it's the best water anywhere in eastern Montana.

The rock that stood up to the millions of years of wind and rain now makes up the strangely shaped formations that can be found at Medicine Rocks State Park.

"For millions of years, the wind has sculpted the soft sandstone into many strange and bizarre shapes that, like shifting clouds, almost overwhelm the imagination," reads a Montana Roadside Geology sign at the park's entrance.

"It's just a really pretty area and very unique," said Doug Habermann, eastern region parks manager for Montana State Parks. "Those rocks, I think you could look at them from every angle in every season and see something different."

The park features a road that winds through the rock outcroppings and takes visitors to camping and picnic areas. On foot, visitors can see even more, wandering through the rocks, climbing into caves and hiking through the surrounding prairie and forests.

"It's a photographer's playground," Habermann said.

The Medicine Rocks are an important cultural site for Native Americans. The area has served as a vision quest site, meeting place and as a lookout to spot enemies and bison.

Montana's earliest settlers also were fascinated by the unique rock formations.

Famed pioneer photographer Evelyn Cameron took photos of the outcroppings, and the Carter County Museum in nearby Ekalaka displays numerous historic photos of the area, including some of settlers picnicking near the rocks.

In 1883, Theodore Roosevelt visited the Medicine Rocks.

"Over an irregular tract of gently rolling sandy hills ... were scattered several hundred detached and isolated buttes or cliffs of sandstone ... caves, columns, battlements, spires and flying buttresses were mingled in the strangest confusion," Roosevelt commented. "Altogether it was as fantastically beautiful a place as I have ever seen."

Mehling has found many names of early settlers and cattle drivers carved into the rocks, along with the dates they passed through. The earliest Mehling has found is from 1885.

"Some of them are initials, some of them are names," he said.

Mehling made a list of names accompanying dates before 1900. That list is housed in the Carter County Museum.

Rocks inside the park are now graffitied with more modern carvings, but a visitor still can find some pre-1900 carvings.

The park includes 12 campsites, many of which are nestled among the rock formations.

Camping among the formations enhances the experience of Medicine Rocks State Parks.
MONTANA STATE PARKS PHOTO

One of the first tourists to visit the area, future president Theodore Roosevelt described what became Medicine Rocks State Park thusly: "As fantastically beautiful a place as I have ever seen."

The sandstone formations are a shocking contrast to the rolling prairie that surrounds them.

Erosion has carved the sandstone at Medicine Rocks State Park.

Photographers love Medicine Rocks State Park for its interesting textures, colors and contrasts.

STATE PARK
FACILITIES

	Nearest Town	Camping	Online Camping Reservations	Flush Toilets
Glacier Country				
Les Mason	Whitefish			
Whitefish Lake	Whitefish	X	X	X
Lone Pine	Kalispell			X
North Shore				
Logan	Libby	X	X	X
Lake Mary Ronan	Dayton	X	X	
West Shore	Lakeside	X	X	
Wayfarers	Big Fork	X	X	X
Big Arm	Polson	X	X	X
Wild Horse Island	Polson			
Yellow Bay	Big Fork	X		X
Finley Point	Polson	X	X	X
Thompson Falls	Thompson Falls	X	X	
Placid Lake	Seeley Lake	X	X	X
Salmon Lake	Seeley Lake	X	X	X
Fish Creek	Alberton			
Frenchtown Pond	French Town			X
Council Grove	Missoula			
Milltown	Missoula			
Travelers' Rest	Lolo			X
Beavertail Hill	Clinton	X	X	X
Fort Owen	Stevensville			
Painted Rocks	Darby	X		
Southwest Montana				
Granite Ghost Town	Philipsburg			
Lost Creek	Anaconda	X		
Anaconda Smoke Stack	Anaconda			
Bannack	Dilon	X	X	X

Showers	Vault toilets	RV Hookups	Boat Launch	Water	Picnic Shelter	Visitor Center	Gift Shop
	X						
X			X	X	X		
	X			X	X	X	X
X		X	X	X	X		
	X	X	X	X			
	X	X	X	X			
X	X	X	X	X	X		
X	X		X	X	X		
	X						
	X		X	X	X		
	X	X	X	X			
	X		X	X	X		
X	X	X	X	X	X		
X	X	X	X	X	X		
	X			X	X		
	X			X			
	X			X	X	X	X
	X			X	X		
	X						
	X		X		X		
	X			X			
	X			X	X	X	X

	Nearest Town	Camping	Online Camping Reservations	Flush Toilets
Clark's Lookout	Dillon			
Beaverhead Rock	Twin Bridges			
Lewis & Clark Caverns	Whitehall	X	X	X
Elkhorn	Elkhorn			
Spring Meadow Lake	Helena			X
Black Sandy	Helena	X	X	X
Yellowstone Country				
Missouri Headwaters	Three Forks	X	X	X
Madison Buffalo Jump	Three Forks			
Greycliff Prairie Dog Town	Greycliff			
Cooney	Roberts	X	X	X
Central Montana				
Smith River	White Sulphur Springs	X	PERMIT REQUIRED	
Tower Rock	Cascade			
First Peoples Buffalo Jump	Ulm			X
Giant Springs	Great Falls			X
Sluice Boxes	Belt	X*		
Marias River	Shelby	X		
Ackley Lake	Hobson	X		
Southeast Montana				
Chief Plenty Coups	Pryor			X
Lake Elmo	Billings			X
Pictograph Cave	Billings			X
Yellowstone River	Billings			
Rosebud Battlefield	Busby			
Tongue River Reservoir	Decker	X	X	
Pirogue Island	Miles City			
Makoshika	Glendive	X	X	X
Medicine Rocks	Ekalaka	X		
Missouri River Country				
Brush Lake	Dagmar	X	X	
Hell Creek	Jordan	X	X	X

*backcountry camping

Showers	Vault toilets	RV Hookups	Boat Launch	Water	Picnic Shelter	Visitor Center	Gift Shop
	X						
X	X	X		X	X	X	X
	X			X	X		
	X		X	X			
	X		X	X	X	X	
	X						
					X		
X	X		X	X			
	X		X				
	X				X		
	X			X		X	X
	X			X	X		
	X						
	X						
	X		X		X		
	X			X	X	X	X
X	X		X	X	X		
	X			X	X	X	X
	X				X		
	X	X	X	X	X		
	X						
	X			X	X	X	X
	X			X	X		
			X	X			
X	X	X	X	X	X		

FAVORITE
STATE PARKS

Once state parks mostly meant signs on the highways for us, but now they're memories of beautiful landscapes, camping trips, boat launches, hikes and special times with friends and family.

Our most frequently asked question (besides, "When are you going to write a book?") has been, "What's your favorite state park?" We've enjoyed them all, and it was a challenge for each of us to select five favorite parks.

ERIN

5. Pictograph Cave State Park: The highlight of this park is, not surprisingly, the pictographs. There are more than 100 pictographs to view, and I enjoyed imagining what the drawings might represent. As a bonus, the park is located in a beautiful setting about 15 minutes outside of Billings.

4. Wild Horse Island State Park: While this park is a little trickier to get to (a boat is required), it's well worth a visit. The island is home to everything from bighorn sheep to native grasses to old homestead buildings, not to mention a herd of wild horses.

3. Makoshika State Park: If you ever thought the landscape of eastern Montana was flat and boring, Makoshika State Park will change your mind. The huge 11,500-acre park is covered in other-earthly looking terrain and a large network of trails allows visitors to explore the land.

2. Giant Springs State Park: Because I live in Great Falls, Giant Springs State Park is my backyard playground. The main part of the park, home to the spring, is beautiful, but there is so much more to the park. Single-track trails extend for miles along both sides of the Missouri River.

1. Medicine Rocks State Park: Numerous people told us that Medicine Rocks would be a treat to visit. It had been hyped so much by the time we got there that I was sure it could never live up to all the good things we'd heard about it. I was wrong. I think I could have spent days walking through and climbing on the rock formations.

KRISTEN

5. Lost Creek State Park: This state park was one of the surprises of our state park challenge. Oasis is the best way to describe the delightful canyon of trees, wildlife, a creek and the falls.

4. Bannack State Park: Our day in Bannack was one of my favorite days of the year. It's a photographer's wonderland, and I took about 100 pictures an hour. The history is fascinating. The scenery is wonderful. I should have visited long before.

3. Smith River State Park: The epitome of adventure. We shared the park with bears, anglers and canoers who alternated between gushing about the gorgeous canyon and trying to keep it a secret for themselves. Floating from boat camp to boat camp was a fun way to experience the outdoors. Plus, s'mores.

2. Lewis and Clark Caverns: The caverns are amazing and a must-see, but as I've returned it's been the well-kept, conveniently located campground and the lands that make up the park that have drawn me. It's been a handy base for exploration of southwest Montana.

1. Missouri Headwaters State Park: We visited 55 state parks in one year. Now my goal is to visit this state park 55 times, and I'm well on my way. I love the scenery, easy access to the Interstate, significance in Montana geology/history and the way it changes with the seasons.

ABOUT THE AUTHORS

Erin Madison grew up in Golden, Colo., and moved to Montana to attend the University of Montana. From there she found her way to the *Great Falls Tribune* in Great Falls, Mont., where she works as an outdoors writer. She enjoys spending as much free time outside as possible, mountain biking, backpacking, cross-country skiing and snowboarding with her boyfriend Josh and their dog Maggie.

Kristen Inbody was born and raised in Choteau, Mont., where her family farms. Since graduating from the University of Montana, she has worked for newspapers in Alaska, Wyoming, Washington, D.C., and Montana, joining the *Great Falls Tribune* staff as feature writer. Kristen was a Peace Corps volunteer in rural Transylvania, Romania, and continues to explore the world.

Erin, Sunny and Kristen explore Makoshika State Park, their 49th of 55 state parks visited in one year.

stateparks.mt.gov
Explore More.

SUPPORTING
MONTANA'S STATE PARKS

Proceeds from this book benefit Montana's state parks on behalf of Montana's Outdoor Legacy Foundation.

If you wish to make an donation directly to Montana's state parks, visit mtoutdoorlegacy.org.